THE
GIFT

God Gave You More Than You'll Ever Know

Kim Allan Johnson

Pacific Press® Publishing Association
Nampa, Idaho
Oshawa, Ontario, Canada
www.pacificpress.com

Edited by Tim Lale
Designed by Tim Larson
Cover photo by Photonica ®

Copyright © 2000 by
Pacific Press® Publishing Association
Printed in the United States of America
All Rights Reserved

Additional copies of this book may be purchased at
http://www.adventistbookcenter.com

Johnson, Kim Allan, 1947-
    The gift : God gave you more than you'll ever know / Kim Allan Johnson.
     p. cm.
    ISBN 0-8163-1768-2 (pbk.)
    1. Jesus Christ—Biography—Passion Week. 2. Seventh-day Adventists—Doctrines.
I. Title.

BT414.J64 2000
232.96—dc21

                                                                99-048074

01 02 03 04 •7 6 5 4

Praise for *The Gift*

The Gift cuts to the heart of the Christian gospel. People often talk about the cross as an event. But my friend, Kim Johnson, has made it an experience. Through powerful illustrations, vivid language, and careful detail, the scenes of the last several days of Christ's life evoke in the reader a magnified understanding of their reality and meaning. We know Jesus better and can identify with Him more strongly. For me, reading this book helped me understand more clearly the immense cost of my salvation, and I wanted to hold more carefully and reverently, "the gift."

—Benjamin D. Schoun, President,
Atlantic Union Conference

A few weeks ago I read your outstanding book and just wanted you to know what an impact it made. You dealt with the reality of the crucifixion in a way that few authors do. It's pretty easy to gold plate the cross and sing trite little songs about it. But when I realize the incredible sacrifice, I stand in awe. I just want you to know that it was appreciated.

—Jere D. Patzer, President
North Pacific Union Conference

I have read [the] book twice. You were truly inspired by the Holy Spirit when you wrote it! I have been greatly blessed! Some of the pictures you painted deeply troubled my spirit. The book pushed me out of my comfort zone. The depth of suffering that Jesus endured for our salvation was revealed in a way I had never before seen. The gospels have taken on new life for me. Thank you for being used of God to move me closer to Him.

—John Freedman, Ministerial Director,
Washington Conference of SDA

Dr. Luke tells us that as Jesus "explained unto them in all the scriptures the things concerning himself," the disciples on the road to Emmaus found their hearts burning within them. *The Gift* does the same thing by re-telling the Old, Old Story in a way that makes it fresh and new. I know no more useful purpose for a book than this!

—Lee Venden, pastor
Auburn, Washington

Halfway through reading the Introduction I had to pause, close the book, and swallow a large lump in my throat before I could continue reading. Kim Johnson's writing gripped both my mind *and* my heart as he walked me through the many facets of Jesus' sacrifice. I treasure this book because it widens my thinking and deepens my appreciation for the greatest Gift ever given.

— Shelley Schurch

I'm 27 years old. I just started reading *The Gift*. It has been a tremendous blessing to me and an incredible answer to prayer. I've been working as a youth pastor for the past year. As I started preaching, I started wondering if I believed with all my heart what I was sharing. I realized that I knew about Christ's love intellectually, but not with my heart. For several months, I have been praying desperately that God would help me to feel His love down deep in my heart. I wanted to be constrained by the love of Christ. I wanted to be able to comprehend the depth and height of His love. I wanted to be able to say with all my heart, "nothing can separate me from the love of Christ." A couple of nights ago a friend lent me his copy. After reading the first chapter, I really had trouble going to sleep that night as I lay awake thinking about the greatness of His sacrifice for me. I think the book is especially excellent for [those of us] who have grown up in the church all our lives, who have heard so much about law and little about God's amazing love. I have been truly blessed. I praise God!

—Martin H. Kim, youth pastor/missionary

Words fail me and I don't know how to begin. I picked up your book this past week and have only read through half of it, yet it has already been woven into my life and journey as a follower of Christ. Your book took me to the next level of acknowledging just what it cost My Lord to save me.

—Cebastyan Bailey

I have to tell you that it has been a long time since the Lord has spoken to me through a book like He has through yours. Your book has put Christ's life into a perspective that I had never looked at before. I can almost feel the pain that Christ went through for me.

—Roger Gilbert, pastor

Read an excerpt from *The Morning*, Kim Allan Johnson's powerful sequel to *The Gift* on page 160.

Contents

A c k n o w l e d g e m e n t s

This book is lovingly dedicated to my precious wife,
whose encouragement and advice were invaluable,
and to my mother,
who taught me to cherish words and dreams

I would like to thank the following people for investing in my dream of exalting the magnificent sacrifice of the Son of God:

My treasured daughter, Stefanie, whose interest in the sufferings of Christ has deepened and expanded my own.

Céleste perrino Walker, whose guidance and editorial skills gave me confidence to persevere.

Dr. Richard Lesher, who sparked my interest in the atonement way back in college.

Michael Sczekan, who challenged and affirmed my thinking as only a close friend can.

Paul Dixon, Gloria DePalma, and Larry Yeagley, who graciously read interminable rough drafts and offered helpful insights.

Ben Schoun, who provided important and timely mentoring.

Ken Baumgarten, whose expertise in Greek helped me understand important nuances of the biblical texts.

As the author of *The Gift*, I would enjoy hearing from you. Share your reactions and comments by contacting me at the following email address: 102555.1145@compuserve.com—Kim Allan Johnson

Foreword

First, I should tell you that no one asked me to write this foreword (although I have always entertained the secret hope that someone would ask me to write one). I volunteered. And the reason I volunteered is that, well, it's a long story, and this is probably the best place to tell it.

I was cruising along in life (OK, it was more like accelerating at the speed of light), completely oblivious to the existence of a man named Kim Johnson. Then one day I received a letter from Kim, in which he introduced himself and asked if I would consider giving him some advice on being a writer. This simple request led to Kim joining my writing team, "Write On!" as one of my writers.

I read some of Kim's writing and was greatly impressed with how God is using his talents. One of the projects Kim asked me to edit was this book. I have to say that this book, more than any book I have ever read on Christ and His life, touched me and blessed my life. At more than one point it brought me to tears. And in the last set of chapters I could feel God's love around me like a warm blanket as I read. I have been urging people to read it even before it was completely written! Reading this book is like spending time sitting at Jesus' feet, asking all the questions you thought of when you were reading the Bible, and having Him patiently explain everything.

It's walking with Him and perceiving His loneliness. It's feeling frustration at the ignorance and irrational prejudice He dealt with every day. It's trembling at the narrow, jagged path He trod each moment on His way to Calvary. It's cringing at the rejection He faced and writhing at the hateful way He was treated.

Ellen White said, "It would be well for us to spend a thoughtful hour each day in contemplation of the life of Christ. We should take it point by point, and let the imagination grasp each scene, especially the closing ones. As we thus dwell upon His great sacrifice for us, our confidence in Him will be more constant, our love will be quickened, and we shall be more deeply imbued with His spirit. If we would be saved at last, we must learn the lesson of penitence and humiliation at the foot of the cross" (*The Desire of Ages,* p. 83).

In *The Gift* Kim Johnson takes us gently by the hand and leads us through Christ's last days on earth. We see His ministry through the eyes of an insider, as someone who walked with Him. We spend companionable moments and compassionate moments. His sacrifice, His gift, is revealed in all its glory, majesty, and splendor. The spectacle of it will take your breath away and comfort you beyond measure.

And now I'll stop writing and let you read it because the sooner you start, the sooner your life will be blessed.

Shalom,
Céleste perrino Walker

Introduction

- " 'For God so loved the world, that he gave his only begotten Son, that whosoever believeth in him should not perish, but have everlasting life' " (John 3:16, KJV).
- "Thanks be unto God for his unspeakable gift" (2 Corinthians 9:15, KJV).
- "The heart of God yearns over His earthly children with a love stronger than death. In giving up His Son, He has poured out to us all heaven in one gift."[1]
- "Hanging upon the cross Christ was the gospel. . . . This is our message, our argument, our doctrine, our warning to the impenitent, our encouragement for the sorrowing, the hope for every believer. If we can awaken an interest in men's minds that will cause them to fix their eyes on Christ, we may step aside, and ask them only to continue to fix their eyes upon the Lamb of God."[2]

Late one evening as I arrived home from work, my wife met me in the hallway with tears in her eyes and said nervously, "I've got some very bad news."

I took in a quick deep breath, trying to brace myself for her next words, and asked what had happened.

"It's Jeff," she explained. "He was in a terrible car accident today . . . and was killed."

The message hit me like a falling timber, and I slumped against the wall in disbelief and shock. Jeff was the very bright, affable firstborn son of the pastor I had interned under. He had recently graduated with honors from college as a theology major and as president of his class. Following in the footsteps of his dad, he had entered the seminary. Now he was dead, his too-short ministry tragically ended.

Jeff's father later told me that one of the most painful experiences in the wake of that terrible loss was gathering up his son's clothes from his apartment near school. Each precious article was a heartbreaking reminder of the good times together, the special conversations, the hopes and dreams. As he ran his hand slowly over the suit his son wore in the pulpit, tears ran off his cheeks and onto the son's orphaned garment.

Hoping the clothes would now benefit someone else, he brought them to a local welfare depot. He stood at the receptionist's desk with the cherished gifts cradled in his outstretched arms. Before he could explain, the woman glanced up hurriedly at the neat bundle, motioned in a bothered manner toward a jumbled heap at one end of the room and said callously, "Over there."

The father wanted to scream out, "But, lady, don't you understand how important these clothes are?" Instead he turned, lovingly placed his offering on the disheveled pile, then hurriedly made his way out the door, fighting back sobs.

Two thousand years ago another grief-stricken Father brought His priceless Gift to a needy world. Humanity glanced up from more important things, pointed to a hill called Calvary, and said "Put it over there." Jesus' contemporaries failed to fully appreciate the Gift then, and for various reasons we continue to miss its deep significance today.

As a theology major at a Christian college, I heard numerous sermons and lectures that referred to the Cross. I also studied commentaries that explored its meaning. But I soon realized that something important was missing in my own experience. Here was the centerpiece of Christianity, and yet it had a relatively limited impact on my heart. I was grateful for God's provision, but its life-changing power largely eluded me. The apostle Paul refers to the Cross as the *dunamis,* or dynamite, of God, but the Cross did not exactly blow me away.

Jesus' sufferings and death finally came alive when I decided to put theological study aside for a while and simply immerse myself in trying to understand what He endured physically, mentally, emotionally, and spiritually from Gethsemane to the cross. I took the time to walk with Him minute by minute through His entire ordeal, from the garden to His cry of victory, "It is finished." I searched for ways to get inside the Man and feel His pain—the punches and lacerations, the utter loneliness and despair.

Suppose you were trying to describe a rainbow to someone who had never seen one. You could take them to a physics lecture on the refractive properties of light. But a far better approach would be to take them outside after a downpour and let them stare up in wonder at the magnificent arch of color. After the rainbow had worked its magic on their hearts, the lecture certainly would be very helpful. Likewise, theological reflection on the sufferings of Christ can be as sterile as a physicist's fact sheet unless it is prefaced by and founded upon a long look at the reality on which it is based.

Sadly, the atonement can become to us just another religious fact rather than a compelling love story. It can become a cliché-riddled historic event rather than an ever-expanding source of amazement. Wonder can be downgraded to a more sedate, mildewed sense of appreciation. When was the last time you lay awake at night, too captivated by Christ's love to sleep? When was the last time you wrestled with the astonishing cosmic risks involved in Jesus' sacrifice? When was the last time your mind stretched to grasp the many layers of suffering He endured? As the Mount Everest of God's self-revelation, as the fullest demonstration of evil's intent and its consequences this side of the judgment, Calvary should affect our hearts and minds in ways that nothing else can.

The Cross is truly immense in its scope and implications. It impinges on every aspect of God's vast creation. Paul wrote, "And through [Christ] to reconcile to himself all things, whether on earth or in heaven, making peace by the blood of his cross" (Colossians 1:20). Ellen White observes, "The plan of redemption had a yet broader and deeper purpose than the salvation of man. . . . Before all the universe it would justify God and His Son in their dealing with the rebellion of Satan" (*Patriarchs and Prophets*, 68, 69).

No matter how much we have taken Jesus' sacrifice for granted, the Spirit of God can still make our mouths drop open and fulfill Christ's prediction within us, " 'I, if I be lifted up from the earth, will draw all men unto Me' " (John 12:32, KJV). *This book is primarily an attempt to portray the rainbow of Jesus' pain and love.* It will hopefully take us a few more steps on that all-important, intensely personal spiritual journey toward knowing God, whom to know is life eternal.

"Then I looked, and I heard the voice of many angels around the throne, the living creatures, and the elders; and the number of them was ten thousand times ten thousand, and thousands of thousands, saying with a loud voice: 'Worthy is the Lamb who was slain to receive power and riches and wisdom, and strength and honor and glory and blessing' " (Revelation 5:11, 12, NKJV).

---

1. Ellen G. White, *Steps to Christ* (Nampa, Idaho: Pacific Press®, 1956), 21.
2. *Seventh-day Adventist Bible Commentary* (Hagerstown, Md.: Review and Herald, 1957), 7-A:662.

Chapter 1

The Traveler

Only fifteen feet ahead of me stood the most important political leader in our state. Glancing around the ornate office, my eight-year-old eyes focused on the oversized mahogany desk. A two-foot-wide green blotter trimmed in light brown leather was flanked by a phone with at least five hundred buttons, a golden pen set, four oak picture frames, an in-box with letters, and a nameplate that read "Governor Volpe." I jammed both hands deep into my suit pockets, fingered the familiar Gumball and miniature dinosaur, and kept shuffling forward in line.

My uncle Al had just been sworn in as Chief Justice of the Massachusetts Superior Court, and relatives and friends turned out in force to congratulate him. His wide shoulders, square jaw, and full-length judge's robe matched his new position of lofty authority and power. He stood next to the governor in a receiving line, smiling broadly and introducing people to Governor Volpe by name. I felt my knees weaken when my turn finally came. All I can remember is my uncle saying, "This is my eight-year-old nephew, Kim Johnson." The governor bent over, shook my sweaty hand, and said, "Nice to meet you, Jim." His calling me "Jim" was the only downer in an otherwise exhilarating day. I didn't feel comfortable correcting him.

After that ceremony I never looked at my uncle in quite the same way again.

To me he had simply been my cousins' quiet dad, who fished, gardened, and worked uptown. Now I had seen his other, grander side, and I admired him in a new and deeper way.

And it is in fact the grander side of Christ that helps me appreciate His sacrifice the most. For years I identified mainly with the meek and mild Jesus. I felt drawn by His gentle spirit. Now, however, I have discovered a deeper love for the Son of God by also focusing on His awe-inspiring side, the cosmic aspect of Him that pulsates with mind-boggling glory and power. This portrait of Christ as the Mighty One has opened up whole new avenues to me for valuing His suffering and death.

One of the biggest challenges we face in talking about Jesus' sacrifice is finding ways to help people sense how awesome it is, when we live in a world where nothing seems truly awesome anymore.

You can now purchase a "gigantic" soft drink at our local convenience store. It used to be simply labeled "large." Same amount of liquid, same container, but this new label is supposed to make it sound tons bigger than the competition. Maybe next week it'll be "colossal." If this trend continues, we'll have just two classifications in life for everything from bagels to light bulbs—"enormous" and "very enormous."

I don't mean to sound picky. But if we keep on using special words to describe common, everyday things, we won't have anything left to use when it really needs to count. If the latest TV show was "totally awesome," what are we supposed to say to describe God?

So, what can help? *Jesus' grander side becomes more real to me by (1) picturing His life before the Incarnation and (2) examining the size of His universe.*

1. Christ's life before the Incarnation

The Jesus we know best was born in Bethlehem. He looked like us; ate, slept, sweated, and got nasty splinters like us. He probably stood no more than 5' 9" tall, with shoulder-length black hair, brown eyes, dark olive skin, black beard, and captivating smile. But within that quite ordinary-looking human body there somehow coexisted another astonishing side of Christ, the side of Him who made everything and who ruled the galaxies and existed from all eternity.

For trillions of years before sin the rest of the universe only knew Jesus as the exalted second member of the Trinity. Angels and unfallen beings responded to Him in awe and adoring worship. Their hearts thrilled with joy at the mere mention of His name.

We can see glimpses of that former life during His ministry on earth. Ellen White says that on the Mount of Transfiguration He prayed that the disciples would "be given a manifestation of the glory He had with the Father before the world was."[1] "And he was transfigured before them, and his face shone like the sun, and his garments became white as light" (Matthew 17:2). Later, as He approached Gethsemane the night He died, Christ referred to His former grandeur. " 'And now, O Father, glorify thou me with thine own self with the *glory which I had with thee before the world was*' " (John 17:5, KJV, italics supplied).

Almost all the stories we have of Christ come from the years He spent on earth as a carpenter and itinerant rabbi. Long before His birth in Bethlehem, the rest of the cosmos could recount story after marvelous story of Christ's activities as God. Ellen White comments on the perspective of unfallen beings:

> That He who had *passed from star to star, from world to world*, superintending all, by His providence supplying the needs of every order of being in His vast creation—that He should consent to leave His glory and take upon Himself human nature, was a mystery which the sinless intelligences of other worlds desired to understand.[2]

Imagine with me for a few moments the planet Elkon, somewhere in the vastness of interstellar space, and try to imagine what it might have been like to be visited by Christ thousands of years before Lucifer's rebellion.

The much-respected inhabitants of planet Elkon eagerly began to gather on Saturday morning in their splendid capital city. An air of expectancy gripped every heart. Today would be a very high day. Christ the King and His angels were coming to celebrate Sabbath with these highly intelligent, generous beings. After assembling in their capital, the Elkonites planned to journey together to a carefully selected place of worship—the vast, breathtaking Valley of Joy. They wanted to arrive early to greet their honored guests. The grand entourage from distant heaven was expected to be there about two hours after sunrise, traversing the fifty trillion miles of interstellar space in mere seconds.

Trannin, a member of Elkon's Supervising Council, watched other citizens arrive in preparation for the trek. Several magnificent structures, widely spaced, dominated the metropolitan area. The centerpiece, the Grand Hall, was a clear, hollowed-out diamond over seventy stories high. Its countless sparkling facets refracted continuously changing colors. Seven rivers met at the center of downtown then surged outward to the east. Thousand-foot-high trees, growing at each corner of the city, bent over until their tips touched, forming a natural canopy of green. Sitting on a bench in Windsong Gardens, Trannin turned his face into the warm morning starlight and meditated on the kindness of the Trinity.

Suddenly the trumpet choir sounded the signal to leave. A dense flock of large, yellow, eight-winged birds passed overhead as if to beckon the people upward. Trannin sprang to his feet. By simply focusing his thoughts on flying, he effortlessly rose into the clear, inviting sky along with a million other inhabitants, all clad in garments of emerald green light.

The Valley of Joy lay due north, about three thousand miles away, in an area not yet inhabited. Foregoing instantaneous thought-travel in order to enjoy the journey, the assemblage of Elkonites stretched out beyond the horizon in an immense square, traveling only at the speed of sound. Trannin turned to the person next to him on the outer edge of the formation and remarked, "Worshipping with heavenly beings is an incredible experience. The way they praise the King is profoundly moving." He turned his face forward again, smiling broadly, and added, "I'm thrilled that they are coming here today!"

Soon the Valley loomed before them, and the entire gathering started to descend. As he neared the ground, Trannin swung his legs gracefully downward and stepped gently onto a sprawling carpet of tiny, fluorescent blossoms. They felt like a soft cushion under his feet. He paused to take in the splendor of the scene.

Far in the distance a majestic mountain range completely ringed the Valley, with peaks stretching upward beyond view. Regularly spaced, two-thousand-foot waterfalls plummeted off the cliffs into a frothing river below. The spray from each waterfall created a series of tall rainbows and filled the air with refreshing moisture. Between the waterfalls, large vines hung from each rock face like immense wall hangings reaching nearly to the ground. Roselike flowers, from one to three feet across, adorned the vines' swirling greenery. The brilliant colors migrated from one flower to the next, mixing and blending into intricate, kaleidoscopic hues. The rest of the landscape opened into an immense meadow dotted near the edges by groves of evergreen trees. Trannin took in a deep draft of invigorating air then reached up and brushed back the hair that had fallen across his forehead.

At the sound of distant music, all eyes turned in the same direction. About forty-five degrees above the horizon, a small circle of light became visible, expanding and intensifying as it neared. Within seconds an angelic choir came into view. Clad in maroon garments with a wide purple fringe, the angels gathered overhead and burst into intricate harmonies, singing "Glory to our beloved

Lord, King of all creation, gracious Source of all life and love." The Elkonites spontaneously responded as one person with their own beautiful chorus of praise.

A trumpet fanfare rang out, and the angels paused then sang, "Blessed is the coming of the exalted One," repeating the phrase seven times, increasing the volume with each repetition. Trannin looked up in time to see the choir forming into a long corridor. His gaze was drawn to the far open end. A different order of angels entered the corridor, taller than the rest, wearing golden garments with a broad blue sash. About five hundred rows deep and three hundred wide, these noble beings descended to the meadow, stood in concentric circles around the citizens of Elkon, then turned their smiling faces upward.

There followed about sixty thousand representatives from nearby galaxies, dressed in the colored lights of their own particular solar system. Lucifer, whose rebellion lay one million years in the future, appeared with Gabriel and seven hundred distinguished administrative officials from heaven. They all touched down in the Valley, forming a vast outer circle, then eagerly looked skyward.

The faraway waterfalls rumbled in low tones, and a delightful feeling of suspense pervaded the scene. Thirty large-plumed, turquoise birds fluttered by.

Trannin caught the approach of another angel choir far more numerous than the first. They were singing praises to Christ. As they neared, other beings, shrouded in yellow light, also became visible, playing a great variety of specially made instruments. Songs of praise filled the Valley, eventually reaching such compelling richness and beauty that Trannin could feel his heartbeat quicken and the hairs on the back of his neck tingle. Tears of delight welled up in his eyes as he became enveloped in the captivating, uplifting sound.

Then . . . silence. Utter peace and calm, lasting about one full minute. Again the singular phrase rang out, echoing loudly across the Valley, "Blessed is the coming of the exalted One." Directly overhead there suddenly appeared the magnificent form of the King, regal and awe-inspiring. Jesus' presence bathed the entire Valley in brilliant, dazzling white light. Mountains lighted up as if ablaze. Every tree, flower, and leaf glowed like a sun. The waters appeared as rivers of undulating light. The air itself seemed to glimmer. At first Trannin shaded his eyes and squinted then easily adjusted.

Immediately the full choir and instruments burst into great anthems of praise, building to a glorious crescendo. While they held the final, impossibly high note, the entire sky exploded into a hundred sunrises. Wave after wave of brilliant reds, yellows, oranges, and purples erupted overhead. A thousand trumpets added their own fanfare of praise. Numerous bolts of lightning flashed from one end of the Valley to the other. The ground trembled. Electricity crackled. Thunder rolled across the sky. Howling winds swirled nearby. The dramatic display continued until Trannin felt that his heaving chest would burst.

Transfixed, the Elkonites let out involuntary gasps. Everyone in the meadow below spontaneously bowed. Trannin bent deeply at the waist, tingling with joy and wondering what might come next.

Once more, complete stillness fell over the scene. Then the sweetest sound in the entire universe, the tender, tenor voice of Jesus declared, "Lift up your heads, my beloved, and lift up your hearts in love." Trannin felt as if the King had spoken directly to him. All eyes turned upward once again, and everyone, angels and unfallen beings, joined as one voice in the anthem, "Blessed is our God, Lord of every living thing, Friend of all creation."

Jesus descended in grandeur into the midst of the eager, awaiting throng. He walked among the Elkonites, exchanging hugs, then gradually made His way toward a high prominence in the middle of the Valley. Everyone pressed closer. After ascending the hill, He addressed the vast gathering, expressing how much the Trinity loved each of them and how He rejoiced that the entire universe was one. "You are my precious children," He said with arms outstretched. "Please know that I would do anything, anything, to preserve your eternal happiness and joy. Let us worship together on this glorious Sabbath day."

2. The Size of Christ's Universe

The second way I have learned to appreciate the grander side of Christ is by understanding the size of His creation.

My best friend in high school, Charlie Fuller, and I used to lie out on the front lawn at night, gazing up at the stars. Our conversation was simple yet profound.

"Hey, Charlie."

"What?"

"Where do you think the universe ends?"

"I dunno."

"You think it just goes on and on and on and on and on . . . forever?"

"Yup."

No one could sum up complex concepts better than Charlie could. With that insightful "yup" he acknowledged something that makes absolutely no sense to our puny human brains—infinite space. Yet there it is, night after night, right above our heads to look at and wonder. And, as the song goes, Jesus made it all. The bigger the universe, the greater the Creator.

In our imagination, let's suppose that I plan to take an incredible journey as an amateur astronaut. Enthusiastic but utterly untrained, I phone "Rent a Rocket" and lease a ten-story-high spaceship to travel into the distant reaches of the universe and visit far-flung galaxies beyond our own Milky Way. On launch day I eat a power breakfast of pancakes, Special-K brand cereal, muffins, bananas, strawberries, and juice. Around 9:00 A.M., technicians strap me into the cockpit and check dozens of dials glowing overhead. They point to a big red button marked "Emergency Exit" and warn, "Better not touch that one by mistake."

I blast off in a roar of flame, and within minutes I'm circling the earth. Anxious to visit the stars, I steer out of orbit and push the throttle ahead to the maximum of 25,000 miles per hour, the same speed as the astronauts who went to the moon. My old Chevy wagon couldn't do much more than 65 miles per hour downhill, so I'm impressed.

Weeks and months roll by, doing endless crossword puzzles and knitting python-sized scarves. Surprisingly, after fifteen years of travel, I'm only at planet Pluto.[3] Major frustration sets in. All this time and I'm only at the outer edge of our own puny solar system. I radio NASA. "Hello, Houston Space Center. Johnson here. I'm supposed to be exploring interstellar space, but I may have to scale back my plans. I guess I'll just stay within our own galaxy. Tell me, how many more months until I get to the very nearest star beyond our sun, Alpha Centauri?" Houston radios back, "Bad news, sir. That should take you a little over 100,000 years, give or take a few decades." Suddenly I feel extremely small and make a hasty U-turn for home. Everything in space is big and far, beyond comprehending.

Actually the universe is so huge that the only reasonable way to measure distances is by figuring how long it would take light to get there. Light screams along at an incredible 186,000 miles per *second*. That translates to an astonishing 670 million miles per hour! To get some idea of how fast that really is, imagine an unusual gun that shoots bullets that travel at the speed of light. If I go out in my backyard and point that gun straight out in front of me and fire it, the bullet would travel around the earth and go through me seven times before I could jump out of the way! Or, to use another analogy, light could go across the United States and back thirty-one times in one second, or the snap of a finger.

Even at that incomprehensible speed, light from outer space takes a very long time to reach the earth. The light that we see right now from our neighboring star, Betelgeuse, left that star about a decade before Columbus set sail for America.[4] Light from Andromeda, the nearest galaxy to ours, takes more than two million years to get here.[5] It takes billions of years for the light from the farthest known galaxies to reach an astronomer's bloodshot eyeball.

There are many more stars than there are grains of sand on all the beaches of the world,[6] yet each of those far-flung fireballs is so far apart that the universe is mostly empty space. If you randomly chose an area of the cosmos the size of a box 6 trillion miles long on each side, the chances of there being a star within that immense space would only be about 1 per cent.[7] Imagine that two galaxies collide. The space between the stars is so vast that there is virtually no chance that any of the stars would hit each other.[8]

Most stars are immense pyrotechnic furnaces. Terence Dickinson provides a graphic description of our own sun: "In essence, the sun is a giant nuclear furnace. At its core, 655 million tons of hydrogen is fused into 650 million tons of helium every second, at a temperature of 27 million degrees Fahrenheit. . . . Five million tons of matter are converted into 400 trillion trillion watts of energy in the process" every second.[9] When a solar flare arcs out into space, it releases the energy of 10 million hydrogen bombs.[10] Hot stuff! Our sun is certainly impressive, but there is a star called a red supergiant that is 800 times larger.[11]

The more we understand the immensity of Christ's creation, the more we can appreciate the astonishing transformation He experienced when He traveled to this earth to become a human being. I have heard people try to describe Christ's incarnation by saying it would be similar to a human being becoming an ant. No way! Not even close. Human beings and ants are practically kissing cousins compared to the differences between God and us. We were made in God's image, but that doesn't make us little Gods. We have much in common with the Trinity, but there are essential differences and huge dissimilarities, not just in size but in kind.

- God has life in Himself. Each breath we take is a gift.
- He had no beginning. Absolutely everything in our backwater world had a starting point.
- He is infinitely powerful and all-knowing. Our minds can't even figure out how our own minds work.

"The more we reflect upon [the Incarnation] the more amazing does it appear. How wide is the contrast between the divinity of Christ and the helpless infant in Bethlehem's manger! How can we span the distance between the mighty God and a helpless child? Far higher than any of the angels, equal with the Father in dignity and glory, and yet wearing the garb of humanity."[12]

In writing to his close friends in Philippi, the apostle Paul dwelt on the stunning condescension of Christ in becoming Man and then being crucified.

Imprisoned at Rome, the intrepid apostle paced back and forth in a dank, dismal room and dictated some of the most sublime, poetic phrases ever employed to describe the indescribable. He begins with the divine side of Christ, "who, though he was in the form of God, did not count equality with God a thing to be grasped" (Philippians 2:6). The Greek word translated "form" means the very essence of something, what it is at the core. Paul says that even though Christ was truly God, He did not grasp onto or insist on maintaining that position of equality with the other members of the Godhead. He stepped off the throne and climbed down the very long ladder into humanity's woe. Paul marks the key steps Christ took as He went from the greatest to the very least:

- "but emptied Himself,
- "taking the form of a servant [slave],
- "being born in the likeness of men.
- "And being found in human form he humbled himself
- "and became obedient unto death,
- "even death on a cross" (Phil 2:7, 8).

I can imagine Paul wincing as he uttered that last phrase, "even death on a cross." Perhaps he paused and stared out the window for a long time as those words hung in the air. Five words that still make the mouths of angels drop open. Our wonderful God hung about three feet above the earth, drenched in His own blood, screaming out for His Father.

The central word in all these verses is *emptied.* William Barclay observes, "It can be used of . . . pouring something out, until there is nothing left."[13] Jesus emptied Himself to the point of being totally dependent on the Father for spiritual strength. He did not use His divinity on His own behalf. He said plainly, " 'The Son can do nothing of himself' " (John 5:19, KJV). He ultimately emptied Himself to the point of dying the death that we deserve.

Paul's mind fast-forwards to a very different scene. He perhaps smiles knowingly as he speaks of the exaltation Christ receives because He gave Himself so fully. "Therefore, God has highly exalted him and bestowed on him the name which is above every name, that at the name of Jesus every knee should bow, in heaven and on earth and under the earth, and every tongue confess that Jesus Christ is Lord, to the glory of God the Father" (Philippians 2:9-11). Jesus' new name is "Lord," a name that Paul predicts will one day be uttered by the entire creation, both good and evil. It is a name Jesus richly deserves for having lived out the principle of selfless servanthood in such dramatic, breathtaking fashion.

His is the greatness of unlimited giving.

From King of kings He became the scum of Judea. At our Lord's trials, foolish man put his haughty foot on Jesus' neck and raised his fist in triumph over the One who created the stars. What ridiculous irony for human beings to think that they had conquered the itinerant Teacher, the One with enough power within Himself to create an entirely new universe. Ellen White comments, "[Christ] knew that in a moment, by the flashing forth of His divine power, He could lay His cruel tormentors in the dust. This made the trial the harder to bear."[14] She adds, "It was as difficult for him to keep the level of humanity as for men to rise above the low level of their depraved natures. . . .Christ was put to the closest test requiring the strength of all His faculties to resist the inclination when in danger, to use His power to deliver Himself from peril."[15]

The Savior set aside His transcendent power to let arrogant sinners drive rusty spikes through His hands and feet. It is shocking enough to contemplate the Man Jesus Christ hanging on a cross. It is far more shocking to watch Him there and know you are looking into the eyes of God.

1. Ellen G. White, *The Desire of Ages* (Nampa, Idaho: Pacific Press®, 1940), 420, 421.
2. Ellen G. White, *Patriarchs and Prophets* (Nampa, Idaho: Pacific Press®, 1958), 69.
3. Herbert Friedman, *The Amazing Universe* (Washington, D.C.: National Geographic Society, 1975), 32.
4. Roy A. Gallant, *Our Universe* (Washington, D.C.: National Geographic Society, 1986), 222.
5. Terence Dickinson, *The Universe and Beyond* (Camden East, Ontario: The Camden House, 1992), 15.
6. Ibid., 67.
7. Ibid., 105.
8. Ibid., 94, 95.
9. Ibid., 71, 75.
10. Gallant, *Our Universe,* 56.
11. Ibid., 227.
12. Ellen G. White, *Signs of the Times,* 30 July 1896.
13. William Barclay, *The Letters to the Philippians and Colossians* (Philadelphia: Westminster Press, 1975), 36.
14. *The Desire of Ages*, 700.
15. Ellen G. White, *Confrontation* (Hagerstown, Md.: Review and Herald, 1971), 85.

Chapter 2

The Gathering Storm

The word *hurricane* often brought back dreadful memories for my father. In 1938, when there were no weather warning devices to speak of, a killer hurricane had clawed its way up the East Coast toward the small town where my dad worked as a full-time firefighter. He remembers gazing up at the ominous, unusually dark sky. Then, within minutes, torrential rains deluged the area, whipped by winds that escalated to a howling one hundred thirty miles per hour. Water five feet deep washed through the firehouse. After the hurricane moved away, my father pulled several bodies out of a home that had been washed into the sea.

As a boy, I remember the pervasive sense of alarm that accompanied the meteorologist's announcement that a hurricane was headed our way. Our family immediately went into storm mode. Candles and lanterns were readied. Lawn items were put inside and windows secured. My dad and I then helped bring in yachts from the local marina. We usually left our own little boat triple-anchored out in the harbor and hoped for the best. Huddled at home as the beast approached, we would wonder how bad it would turn out to be.

Jesus was no stranger to fierce winds and high seas. He had this wonderful habit of turning them all into gentle summer breezes. But another kind of storm burst upon Him that was not so easily tamed, a *storm of hate* that swirled about Him during His ministry and eventually culminated in His death. As His ministry unfolded, the storm of hostility gathered strength and escalated to a furious, howling hurricane during the final week of His life. "From the desert to Calvary, the storm of Satan's wrath beat upon Him, but the more mercilessly it fell, the more firmly did the Son of God cling to the hand of His Father, and press on in the bloodstained path."[1]

Following the main elements of that storm over the course of Christ's public ministry can help us appreciate more fully the enormous difficulties He faced as He sought to save our planet. We see the horrendous pressures under which He had to operate. Those pressures built to withering proportions, reaching a crescendo during the final week of His ministry. By tracking that storm, we also discover new dimensions of His love.

Artists know that the way to make light colors brighter is to paint them next to the darkest hues. Likewise, Jesus' love stands out in dramatic fashion as it is contrasted with the animosity of fallen human beings. By reflecting on the hate that Christ endured, we can also gain a much deeper admiration of His phenomenal courage. It took lionhearted heroism and fearlessness to walk head-on into the dangerous situations He faced over and over again during His tumultuous ministry.

First cleansing of the temple: John 2:12-22

Upwards of one hundred thousand people from near and far jammed into Jerusalem and its environs for the first Passover since Jesus' baptism. The Savior made His way inconspicuously to the city as part of a large caravan of pilgrims.[2] Passing through the thick outer walls of the capital, His eyes fell upon the glittering temple precincts. The magnificent layout consisted of a series of descending courtyards in concentric circles, each forming a separate area of worship. Nearest the temple was the Court of the Priests, surrounded by the Court of the Israelites, then the Court of the Women, and finally the Court of the Gentiles. Non-Jews could only worship in this outermost area. Signs promised the death penalty if they ventured closer.

It was here, in the Court of the Gentiles, that many entrepreneurs had set up shop to ply their nefarious trade and suck every possible dime out of the struggling populace. The place became a haven for con artists, greedy money-changers, and sellers of oxen, sheep, and doves. Any attempt at prayer or meditation was overwhelmed by the uproar of barter and angry disputes. The bedlam was not unlike the floor of the New York Stock Exchange.

William Barclay observes that "this business of buying and selling belonged to the family of Annas who had been High Priest."[3] Annas and his relatives raked in immense sums from the national feasts, skimming off a percentage of every underhanded transaction. They sustained an opulent lifestyle at the expense of tens of thousands of innocent worshipers. Life for the high priest was very, very good. The abuses were well-known and widely resented by the multitudes, but no one dared confront the deeply entrenched, long-standing status quo. Through harsh intimidation and skillful politicking, powerful Jewish leaders made sure that nobody disturbed their well-oiled money machine. Attempts at reform would be like trying to clean up the mob in Chicago during the 1930s.

Jesus stood at the edge of the Court of the Gentiles and took in the entire scene. Indignation and hurt welled up within Him. The noisy racket denied thousands of non-Jews the only place they could come to worship the true God. Christ's penetrating eyes swept over the long lines at the many busy booths and stalls. Slowly, inexplicably, every head turned and became riveted upon the arresting stare of this youthful Galilean. Every sound was hushed. "The silence becomes painful. A sense of awe overpowers the assembly."[4]

Divine love compelled the Savior to act. He picked up a whip of small cords and held it menacingly over His head as He slowly descended the gleaming marble steps. He pushed His way through the tightly packed crowd, grabbed the ornate, silk-covered table of a money-changer, and with one mighty heave flung it ten feet across the pavement, sending tall stacks of coins spinning and clinking across the floor. Then another table, and another. John tells us that "he drove them all out of the temple" (John 2:15, KJV). The animals fled before His scourge, bleating and groaning. Doves fluttered up from opened cages. Panic broke out as everyone fought for the exits.

"Overpowered with terror, the priests and rulers had fled from the temple court, and from the searching glance that read their hearts. In their flight they met others on their way to the temple, and bade them turn back, telling them what they had seen and heard."[5]

The Jewish leaders milled around outside like frightened school children during their first fire drill. Embarrassment, bewilderment, and raw hatred now surged within them. From the priest's perspective, this one lone Carpenter, *in His first public act in Jerusalem*, had made utter fools of them all. The family of Annas the high priest was particularly alarmed because Christ had hit them where it hurt the most, in their wallet, disrupting their source of wealth. Is it any wonder that we read, "As the priests and rulers returned to the temple, they had proposed to kill Jesus, and thus rid themselves of the troubler."[6]

The storm was already producing ominous rumbles of thunder.

Paralytic at the Pool of Bethesda: John 5:1-15

Healing the paralytic at the Pool of Bethesda was a watershed event in Jesus' ministry. For the first time He openly challenged the oppressive Sabbath rules of the Jews.[7] Talk about taking on a "sacred cow!" These countless man-made regulations were at the very heart of Israel's national identity. They were the bulwark that separated the meticulous Pharisees from the unholy Israeli masses. Jesus knew full well that breaking these fabricated Sabbath requirements would dramatically ratchet up the hatred of His enemies, but He did it to draw people into a discussion of true Sabbath keeping.

One day as a young pastor I naively decided, on my own, to move a couple of back pews. The church needed room for more Sabbath School classes, and the sanctuary was never more than 60 percent full anyway. I commandeered two deacons, who helped me store the pews up over the mothers' room. At that week's church board meeting someone raised a hand and asked to speak. He leaned forward, glowered at me as if I'd just murdered his mother, and spat out the angry words, "You call yourself a man of God? How dare you desecrate our beautiful church! What right do you have to go in there and toss pews around, destroying what it has taken us decades to build up? This is outrageous." I leaned back, caught my breath, and nervously pondered the risks of change. The harshness I encountered was child's play compared to the rancor heaped on Christ for daring to tamper with the Pharisees' venerated Sabbath laws.

Jesus decided the time had come to upset the Jewish apple cart in a big way. He strode over to the Pool of Bethesda by the Sheep Gate of the city in order to deliberately challenge the ridiculous Pharisaical rule that no one could be healed on the Sabbath.[8]

At the pool, Christ came upon scores of desperately ill people. "He longed to exercise His healing power, and make every sufferer whole."[9] Instead, He chose only the most heart-rending case, a man paralyzed for thirty-eight long, torturous years. With infinite compassion, Jesus bent over the shriveled man, prostrate on his well-worn, filthy rug, and spoke the life-changing words, "Rise, take up thy bed, and walk" (John 5:8, KJV).[10]

As if it were not mind-boggling enough to the Pharisees that Jesus healed on the Sabbath, He intentionally asked the man to pick up his bed and carry it throughout the city "in order to publish the great work that had been wrought upon him. This would raise the question of what it was lawful to do on the Sabbath, and would open the way for Him to denounce the restrictions of the Jews." [11] Healing and bed-carrying—two major violations in one miracle.

Soon the Jewish leaders located Jesus and hauled Him before the Sanhedrin to answer for His sacrilege. "What right do you have to break our laws!" they snarled. If they were upset before, Christ's answer sent His enemies right through the roof. " 'My Father is working still, and I am working' " (John 5:17). His Father was busy blessing people on Sabbath, and therefore He could do the same. In these carefully chosen words, Christ put Himself on the same level as the Divine. John writes, "This was why the Jews sought all the more to kill him, because he not only broke the Sabbath but also called God his Father, making himself equal with God" (John 5:18). "The fury of the rulers knew no bounds. Had they not feared the people, the priests and rabbis would have slain Jesus on the spot."[12]

Then as if to rub salt in the wound, this self-appointed, renegade Rabbi from Hickville had the insolence to turn on His distinguished accusers and rebuke them for their hard hearts and ignorance of the Scriptures![13] Beside themselves with rage, the Jewish leaders decided to send messengers throughout the country warning people that Jesus was an impostor, demonizing Him as much as possible. It was from the time of this healing at Bethesda that the priests began more formally and consistently to plot the Savior's death.[14] Christ retreated many miles north to the relative safety of mountainous Galilee.

Man with a withered hand: Mark 3:1-6

In Galilee Jesus again had a head-on collision with the Jewish authorities over Sabbath keeping when He bravely entered a local synagogue and ministered to a man with an injured hand. Tradition indicates that the man was a stone mason who now had no means of making a living.[15] The front row of pews were occupied by a delegation of Sanhedrin spies from far-away Jerusalem. Mark tells us, "And He [Jesus] looked around at them with anger, grieved at their hardness of heart" (Mark 3:5).

Knowing the danger to Himself, Christ motioned the wounded man to come forward.[16] Full of kindness, Jesus uttered the wonderful words, " 'Stretch out your hand,' " and it was made completely whole (Mark 3:5).

The Pharisaic spies were so incensed, so enraged, over this Sabbath healing that they immediately formed a league with their lifelong enemies, the Herodians, and plotted "how to destroy him" (Mark 3:6). Christ avoided further trouble by withdrawing to the sea. Three times in the space of three verses Mark mentions the great multitudes that now thronged Jesus' steps from all over Galilee, from Jerusalem, one hundred miles to the south, and even from the foreign cities of Tyre and Sidon (see Mark 3:7, 8). So immense were the crowds, the Savior had to teach from a boat to avoid being trampled on and crushed. The spies no doubt rushed back to Jerusalem with the alarming news that Christ's widespread popularity had reached extraordinary proportions.

Rejection in Galilee: John 6:25-7:1

In the late spring of A.D. 29, Jesus had been bitterly disappointed by the horrible reception He received during His return visit to the synagogue back home in Nazareth. His mother, brothers, and sisters were all there as He spoke, no doubt bursting with pride.[17] But when He told the worshipers they were more hardhearted than some of the heathen, they tried to murder Him by tossing Him off a cliff. A year later, in the early spring of A.D. 30, He returned a final time, and the people rejected Him once again (see Luke 4:16-30; Mark 6:1-6).

Around this same period, after Jesus miraculously fed thousands of people from five small loaves and two measly fish, the excited crowds attempted to make Him king. He sternly rebuked their efforts and disbursed the throngs of people, but the next day they flocked to Him nonetheless. It was then that He plainly stated the spiritual nature of His kingdom, " 'Truly, truly, I say to you, unless you eat the flesh of the Son of man and drink his blood, you have no life in you' " (John 6:53). In effect, He told them, "I am not going to overthrow the Romans. My kingdom is about feeding on the Bread of Life and changing people's hearts." He dashed their hopes of earthly glory, and from that time forward the masses up north turned their backs on Him and treated Him with disdain. "After this many of his disciples drew back and no longer went about with him" (John 6:66). "And thus in Galilee the current of popular feeling was turned against Him, as, the year before, it had been in Judea."[18]

Feast of Tabernacles: John 7:1-15, 30-39

This Feast of Tabernacles is particularly important because it was the first time Jesus attended any of the great national gatherings in Jerusalem after healing the paralytic at the Pool of Bethesda about a year and a half before.[19] During that eighteen-month period, John tells us, "He would not go about in Judea, because the Jews sought to kill Him" (John 7:1). Ellen White adds, "He was hunted by the scribes and the Pharisees, and he fled from town to town, from city to city, to escape their malice, and to preserve his life till his mission should be completed."[20]

At the great feast, faithful Israelites commemorated Israel's wilderness wanderings by dwelling in booths. Despite the disaffection shown several months before in Galilee, hoards of Jewish pilgrims from all over the world journeyed to Jerusalem specifically to see Christ.[21] Excitement eventually reached a fever pitch as thousands wondered whether Jesus dared to make an appearance or if He would once again choose to stay away (see John 7:11). As the expectations of the masses swelled and the nervousness of the authorities intensified, you could cut the tension in the city with a knife.

Meanwhile, the Savior secretly traveled into Jerusalem unnoticed by the crowds. Then, in a breathtaking display of courage, He marched right into the temple court at the height of the festivities and took up a position where everyone could see and hear Him clearly, including the enemies who were thirsting for His life.[22] All eyes turned in His direction. Every voice was hushed as He gazed out over the large gathering. Then His voice sounded like a clarion throughout the temple court, teaching deep and life-changing truths from God's Word.

Bewildered at the reticence of the Jewish leaders, the multitudes said, " 'Is not this the man [Christ] whom they seek to kill? And here he is, speaking openly, and they say nothing to him!' " (John 7:25, 26). The authorities tried to arrest Jesus but were thwarted by angelic intervention. On the last day of the feast, the Pharisees again sent a special delegation to arrest Jesus. The temple posse came back without Him, however, shrugging their shoulders and offering the startling excuse, " 'No man ever spoke like this man!' " (John 7:46). Defeated, the priests threw up their hands and retreated to their homes for the night.

The next day Jesus fearlessly entered the temple court yet again. In another dispute with the Pharisees, He stunned everyone present by declaring, " 'Verily, verily, I say unto you, before Abraham was, I am' " (John 8:58, KJV). Even the common people were shocked at His answer, making Himself equal with God. "Now many of the people, siding with the priests and rabbis, took up stones to cast at Him."[23] Jesus slipped away, but rather than racing out of town, He stayed in the immediate area and sent the priests into orbit yet again by healing a blind man on the Sabbath. With Jerusalem at the boiling point, Christ headed back north into calmer territory.

Last journey to Jerusalem

It was now late autumn in A.D. 30. The time had come for Jesus to make the final journey from Galilee that would eventually put Him on a cross. "His steps are turned toward Jerusalem, where His foes have long plotted to take His life; now He will lay it down. He set His face steadfastly to go to persecution, denial, rejection, condemnation, and death."[24]

Jesus now initiated what was probably one of the greatest advertising campaigns in history. By the time He reached Calvary, He wanted every eye fixed on His sacrifice. The attention of as many people as possible must be drawn to

His suffering and crucifixion. There were two key aspects to His strategy. First of all, He took the most circuitous route possible toward Jerusalem, on a journey of several months, in order to reach the maximum number of people. One is reminded of the whistle-stop presidential campaigns of our own day. Second, He dispatched seventy disciples that He had personally trained earlier in Galilee while the Twelve were on their own missionary tour. "After this the Lord appointed seventy others, and sent them on ahead of him, two by two, into every town and place where he himself was about to come" (Luke 10:1). This advance party would stir up intense interest and expand His influence. Even though the Samaritans had rudely rebuffed Christ, He instructed the seventy to make them their first priority.[25]

Eventually Christ reached Jerusalem in time for the Feast of Dedication, where His words once again provoked a firestorm. He asserted, " 'I and the Father are one' " (John 10:30). The Jews picked up rocks from Herod's building site at the temple and tried to stone Him. This time He quickly retreated east across the Jordan to Perea for several months to let tempers cool.

It is during this period that many of Jesus' famous parables were given. He couched His teachings in parables in order to avoid giving His enemies ground for further accusations.

Jesus did not relish controversy or engage in it unnecessarily, but He was always faithful to the requirements of the saving mission He had to fulfill. The persistent hatred of the Jewish leaders tore at His soul. Rejection caused Him untold grief. We cannot calculate the inner pain the Author of love endured as hostility and rancor dogged His steps.

Raising of Lazarus: John 11:47-54

Jesus' attention was once again drawn to turbulent Jerusalem when He received news a few weeks before Passover that His close friend Lazarus lay extremely ill. The home of Mary, Martha, and Lazarus was in Bethany, only about one and a half miles east of the city. John tells us that Jesus loved this little family, and despite the terrible dangers, Christ told His disciples, " 'Let us go into Judea again' " (John 11:7). Immediately they were thinking, *This is not a great idea!* The Scriptures record their response: " 'Rabbi, the Jews were but now seeking to stone you, and are you going there again?' " (John 11:8).

I attended college in the middle of a large city. Coming back to my apartment one night, I noticed several police cars in the park about one hundred yards from our front door. Their headlights were all pointed toward a blanketed object sprawled on the ground. A spectator informed me that a man had just been murdered minutes before. And I lived in one of the better neighborhoods! Everyone knew there were areas of the city you never entered alone at night. Gangs, racial violence, and muggers made certain streets strictly off limits. If you had any sense at all, you simply stayed away.

I'm sure the disciples felt that same way about returning to Jerusalem. The Jews had already passed an edict that anyone who became a disciple of Christ would be excommunicated.[26] Yet, to their credit, the Twelve eventually relented, and Thomas bravely declared, " 'Let us also go, that we may die with him' " (John 11:16). When Jesus brought four-day-dead Lazarus back to life, the stunning news spread like wildfire.

Events were now gaining an inexorable momentum and, in the view of the Jewish authorities, threatened at any time to spiral out of control. *The raising of Lazarus dramatically fanned the flames of trouble.* Sadducees and Pharisees alike were now desperate for a solution to the Jesus problem. "A meeting of the Sanhedrin was at once called to decide as to what should be done."[27] Nicodemus and Joseph were conveniently omitted. The intense anxiety that pervaded the meeting is revealed by this fear: that if nothing were done, everyone would believe on Christ and the Romans would react to any subsequent uprising by destroying the temple and the very nation itself (see John 11:48). Through impassioned oratory, Caiaphas convinced the members that Jesus must be put to death. They voted to kill Him at the earliest opportunity but delayed executing the sentence for fear of repercussions from the populace (John 11:53).

Jesus knew that His time had not yet come, so He gathered His disciples and slipped away to a town called Ephraim, about fifteen miles north of Jerusalem. The Pharisees quickly issued a warrant for His arrest. "Now the chief priests and the Pharisees had given orders that if any one knew where he was, he should let them know, so that they might arrest him" (John 11:57).

Triumphal entry: Matthew 21:1-11; Mark 11:1-10; Luke 19:29-44; John 12:12-19

Jesus now undertook the last phase of His journey toward suffering and death. Stomach-churning fear gripped the Twelve. "And they were on the road, going up to Jerusalem, and Jesus was walking ahead of them [the disciples]; and they were amazed, and those who followed were afraid" (Mark 10:32). As Christ passed through Jericho, fifteen miles north of Jerusalem, He had ministered to Zacchaeus and healed blind Bartimaeus. Then, six days before the Crucifixion, He made His way to the home of Mary, Martha, and Lazarus in Bethany. Reports of Christ's presence near the city filtered back to the Jewish leaders, whose "rage against Jesus grew more bitter. They could hardly wait for the opportunity of removing Him forever from their way."[28]

On the Saturday evening before Calvary, the priests and Pharisees called an emergency council meeting, during which they confirmed the plan to take Jesus quietly and kill Him as soon as possible. In their vehement hatred and anxious foreboding, they voted to murder Lazarus as well. On this same Saturday night Judas rushed in anger from the feast at Simon's house and went directly to the Jewish council meeting. There he promised to betray Jesus for thirty pieces of silver. He would meet with them again, probably on Tuesday evening, to firm up their plans[29] (see Matthew 26:13-15).

Late Sunday morning the worst fears of the Jewish leaders came true. From their perspective, they could hardly have imagined a more horrible development. Jesus chose to ride into Jerusalem in triumph on the back of a colt, accompanied by thousands and thousands of cheering followers who longed to make Him king. Even though upward of a hundred thousand people were in and around Jerusalem for Passover, so many went out to meet Jesus that hardly anyone was left in the city to attend the evening sacrifice.[30] In utter dismay the Pharisees said to one another, " 'Look, the world has gone after him' " (John 12:19). "Burning with envy and malice," the Pharisees ran out to stop the huge procession, but the best they could manage was a pathetic protest that such noisy demonstrations were against a city ordinance![31] It was like aiming a squirt gun at a raging inferno. As the capstone to the priests' frustration, the Roman officers turned on the Pharisees and charged them with disturbing the peace![32] Some days it just doesn't pay to get up in the morning.

Second cleansing of the temple: Matthew 21:12-16, 23-46; Mark 11:15-19, 27-33; 12:1-12; Luke 19:45-48; 20:1-19

Sunday evening Jesus got away from the crowds, surveyed the temple precincts, then returned to Bethany and spent the rest of the night in prayer. Out of love for His friends and enemies alike, He put together a daring plan to renew true worship at the temple.

Monday morning He did the unthinkable once again by cleansing the Court of the Gentiles for the second time in three years. Just when Annas had gotten his cash cow back to good working order! Divinity flashed through humanity, and the mere look of the Son of God sent everyone scurrying in utter panic. The priests "were now more terrified than before and . . . fled from His presence, driving their cattle before them."[33] Mark adds the interesting historic note that Jesus even told everyone to stop using the temple as a convenient shortcut on their business errands from the eastern part of the city to the Mount of Olives[34] (see Mark 11:16).

At the same time everyone else was fleeing, the children and infirm flocked in the opposite direction, running to get as near to Christ as possible (see Matthew 21:14, 15).

Irate and humiliated, the Jewish leaders "sought a way to destroy him" (Mark 11:18). At this point Jesus seems to have basically taken control of the temple area, teaching and healing as He pleased, until He chose to leave for the final time late Tuesday afternoon. He had silenced the Pharisees and Herodians when they asked, " 'Is it lawful to give tribute unto Caesar, or not?' " and " 'Which is the great commandment in the law?' " (Matthew 22:17, 36, KJV). Next, Jesus checkmated the Sadducees when they asked Him a trick question about the resurrection (see Matthew 22:23ff). With the priests and rulers completely defeated and deflated in the eyes of the people, it is no wonder that Matthew records, "And no one was able to answer him a word, nor from that day did any one dare to ask him any more questions" (22:46).

Tuesday afternoon must have sent the Pharisees reaching for the Maalox brand stomach reliever. In one rebuke after another, Jesus publicly denounced them in order to break the unthinking loyalty of the people. This was also His last desperate attempt to get through to the Jewish leaders themselves. If I saw my two-year-old daughter playing in the middle of a highway, I wouldn't speak to her in gentle tones. I'd shout rather harshly in order to save her life. The Jewish leaders were standing right on the yellow line spiritually, with a huge tractor-trailer bearing down on them. It would not have been loving or appropriate for Jesus to talk to them in gentle tones either. He called the Pharisees " 'hypocrites' " seven times, " 'blind' " five times, not to mention " 'fools,' " " 'whitewashed tombs,' " " 'snakes,' " and " 'a brood of vipers' " (Matthew 23:1-39). "Corresponding to the eight Beatitudes in the Sermon on the Mount with which His public ministry began, He now closed it with eight denunciations of woe."[35]

We must always remember that "He . . . never gave needless pain to a sensitive soul. . . . He spoke the truth always, but in love. When he denounced hypocrisy, unbelief, and iniquity, it was not in tones of thunder; but tears were in his voice as he uttered his scathing rebukes."[36]

The Jewish council met twice that Tuesday to figure out how to crush the outrageous Rabbi[37] (see Matthew 22:15). The full fury of the storm of hate had arrived.

The end

Luke now records Jesus' efforts to warn His disciples about the raw hatred of the Jewish leaders. Behind the scenes terrible forces were at work. In one particularly poignant verse, Jesus said, " 'Let him who has no sword sell his mantle and buy one' " (Luke 22:36). Christ was speaking in figurative language about the need to be on guard spiritually, but the disciples took Him literally and answered, " 'Look, Lord, here are two swords' " (Luke 22:38). One of those very swords would soon be used in Gethsemane to cut off a servant's ear. Thoroughly disgusted with the spiritual blindness of the Twelve, Jesus simply replied, " 'It is enough!' " (Luke 22:38). "Jesus, disappointed at their obtuseness, lets the subject drop."[38]

The situation in Jerusalem was now so extremely dangerous that Jesus had to take some extraordinary precautions. Fearing that Judas might discover the location of the upper room and have Him prematurely arrested, Christ kept the address secret from everyone except Peter and John. He didn't even tell these two trusted disciples about the specific arrangements He had already made. Instead, He simply told them, " 'Behold, when you have entered the city, a man carrying a jar of water will meet you; follow him into the house which he enters' " (Luke 22:10). "To carry water was a woman's task. A man carrying a jar of water would be as easy to pick out as, say, a man using a lady's umbrella on a wet day. This was a pre-arranged signal between Jesus and a friend."[39]

After Jesus was betrayed and arrested, the Jewish leaders finally had Him in their grasp. Many months of pent-up animosity poured forth in torrents. In their indignation they abused the Son of God unmercifully during the trials. They denounced Him bitterly. Before Pilate and Herod they screamed for Christ's crucifixion, the cruelest death possible. Finally the moment arrived that they had dreamed about for so long, when Christ bowed His head on the cross and died. The priests then revealed the depth of their fury by doing something that is reminiscent of an enraged killer who shoots his victim with fifteen bullets when just one would do. The Roman soldiers, who were experts in death, officially pronounced the Savior dead. But the Jewish leaders asked the soldiers to shove a spear through Jesus' bloodied corpse, just to make sure.[40]

---

1. *The Desire of Ages*, 759.
2. Ibid., 154.
3. William Barclay, *The Gospel of Mark* (Philadelphia: Westminster Press, 1975), 274.
4. *The Desire of Ages*, 158.
5. Ibid., 162.
6. Ibid., 164.
7. See *Seventh-day Adventist Bible Commentary* (Hagerstown, Md.: Review and Herald, 1956), 5:949.

8. See *The Desire of Ages,* 206.
9. *The Desire of Ages*, 201.
10. See *The Desire of Ages*, 202.
11. *The Desire of Ages*, 206.
12. Ibid., 208.
13. Ibid., 211.
14. *Seventh-day Adventist Bible Commentary*, 5:950.
15. Barclay, *The Gospel of Mark*, 67.
16. *The Desire of Ages*, 286.
17. Ibid., 236.
18. Ibid., 393.
19. Ibid., 450; *Seventh-day Adventist Bible Commentary*, 5:452.
20. Ellen G. White, "Faith Manifested by Works," *Signs of the Times*, 2 Feb. 1891.
21. *The Desire of Ages*, 451.
22. Ibid., 452.
23. Ibid., 470.
24. Ibid., 486.
25. Ibid., 488.
26. Ibid., 538.
27. Ibid., 537.
28. Ibid., 558.
29. *Seventh-day Adventist Bible Commentary*, 5:517.
30. *The Desire of Ages*, 571.
31. Ibid., 572.
32. Ibid., 581.
33. Ibid., 592.
34. Barclay, *The Gospel of Mark*, 274.
35. Alfred Edersheim, *The Life and Times of Jesus the Messiah* (Grand Rapids, Mich.: Eerdmans, 1974), 2:410, 411.
36. Ellen G. White, "The New Year," *Second Advent Review and Sabbath Herald*, 16 Dec. 1884.
37. *The Desire of Ages*, 593.
38. Norval Geldenhuys, *Commentary on the Gospel of Luke* (Grand Rapids, Mich.: Eerdmans, 1975), 572.
39. William Barclay, *The Gospel of Luke* (Philadelphia: Westminster Press, 1975), 265.
40. *The Desire of Ages*, 772.

Chapter 3

The Pain of Being Misunderstood

A close friend of mine lay severely ill in the local hospital. As the disease progressed, his abilities and freedoms diminished drastically. Bedridden, unable to eat, he finally became so sick that he could no longer even talk clearly. With this last vestige of normalcy snatched from him, his sense of isolation became nearly complete. We communicated through a hit-and-miss system of my asking questions and his moving his head Yes or No.

One day I inquired, "John, what is the hardest part of this whole miserable situation for you?" With tears welling up in his eyes, he slowly pointed to his mouth, and I realized for the first time just how devastating it is to be unable to make yourself understood.

Jesus faced a similar problem, not because of any illness or any deficiency as a communicator but because of the stubbornness and pride of men. His teachings were often totally unintelligible to those around Him. Of all His teachings, none was more misunderstood than the truth that the Messiah must die. The Jews had been taught since childhood that the Messiah would be a conquering hero and overthrow the hated Romans. All Jews gathered strength to endure from the burning conviction that one day their Roman oppressors would be utterly crushed. Any other scenario was totally unthinkable.

Since at least the age of twelve, Christ knew otherwise. Jesus knew that salvation was in His own death, not the death of the Romans. Somehow, some way, He had to get the Jews to understand that there would be a dreadful cross instead of a glorious earthly crown.

In October 1962 the United States and the former Soviet Union came heart-stoppingly close to nuclear war. As Soviet general, Anatoly Gribkov, put it, "Nuclear catastrophe was hanging by a thread . . . and we weren't counting days or hours, but minutes."[1] Premier Nikita Khrushchev had started placing nuclear missiles in Cuba, within range of the United States. President John Kennedy demanded their removal and cordoned off the island to intercept any further military shipments. Tensions mounted nearly to the breaking point, and the incident generated a feeling of white-knuckle suspense. The stakes were enormous. The lives of millions hung in the balance. Finally the issue was resolved, and the world community breathed a deep, collective sigh of relief.

In a very real sense, our topic for this chapter is a far greater suspense story than two countries locking heads over dangerous missiles. The stakes for Jesus were cosmic in scope. The issues were of universal significance. The sense of urgency pressed down upon the Savior with suffocating weight. He had only three and a half years to convince people that He was born to die on a cross. Within that short period of time He had to get people to understand that their long-awaited Messiah was going to "deliver them" by being executed at the hands of the enemy. All evil would be overcome by sacrificial love.

Unless He could change people's minds about His mission, there would be no one to understand, no one to interpret, no one to explain, no one to pass on the gospel story. No Good News. No New Testament. Everything depended on Jesus' ability to break through decades of rock-hard misunderstanding. Everything depended on His ability to get people to accept the very last thing on earth anyone wanted to hear.

So how did Jesus plan to change people's minds about the role of the Messiah? There were two key elements in His strategy: (1) to avoid any personal association with the word *Messiah* and (2) to focus on reeducating a few people. This chapter explores those two crucial goals.

Christ completely avoided any association with the word *Messiah*.

Jesus' struggle to make Himself understood as the One who must suffer is brought out most vividly in the Gospel of Mark. The writer captures Christ's horrendous uphill battle against centuries of false expectations by portraying Him as what some have called the "secret" or "hidden" Messiah.

Since Christ was indeed the long-looked-for Messiah of Bible prophecy, it is reasonable to expect Him to have utilized every possible method to make Himself known as the Messiah and shout it from the rooftops. On the contrary, Jesus never even referred to himself as the Messiah, and when others did so, He strongly urged them to not breathe a word of it.

Mark 3:11 tells us that after Jesus healed a man of an unclean spirit the spirit cried out, " 'Thou art the Son of God [Messiah]!' " You would expect Jesus to say, "Did you hear what that evil spirit just said? He's right, I am the Messiah, the one you've all been looking for!" Instead, Christ "straightly charged them that they *should not make him known*" (verse 12).

In Mark 8:29 Peter experienced a breakthrough revelation when he confessed, " 'Thou art the Christ' " (*Christ* means Messiah in Greek). Again, instead of Jesus saying, "That's right. Now go and tell everyone you know," the Scriptures record, He "charged them that they *should tell no man of him*" (verse 30).

One evening Christ singled out Peter, James, and John to climb a mountain with Him to pray. Christ's new movement seemed to be having a particularly hard time lately, and these three must have wondered if they had made the right decision in signing on. They had given up a very prosperous fishing business amid criticism from friends and relatives, and the disciples now second-guessed that commitment all the way up the darkened slopes. The summit was quiet except for an occasional rustling in the underbrush and the stirrings of a southwest breeze.

Suddenly Jesus stood up from praying and was surrounded by light as dazzling and brilliant as the noonday sun. He was glorified before them. *Oh, if our relatives could only see this!* the disciples thought. *He is the Messiah. Such power and majesty. What a vindication of our decision!*

The three disciples could not contain themselves, and soon, after the glory faded, they turned to rush down the mountain and tell all. But again "He admonished and expressly ordered them to *tell no one what they had seen*" (Mark 9:9, Amplified).

So what's going on here? Why this determined effort to keep Himself from being known as the Messiah? It sounds like just the opposite of what Christ should be doing.

The reason is that the word *Messiah* was soaked with wrong meanings. That word had become synonymous with "Political Conqueror," and Jesus could not allow Himself to be thought of in those terms.

For instance, suppose I introduced a new pastor in your church as someone who liked to be called the Ayatollah. What would be going through your mind?

Even if I said that the title *Ayatollah* originally meant "gentle one," you'd still be thinking of that wacky religious leader over in Iran during the Carter presidency. The same thing had happened to the word *Messiah*, which originally meant "Anointed One." In Jesus' time it meant someone who stomps all over Rome.

Try to imagine how appealing the idea of a political conqueror would have been to the Jews of Jesus' time. The Israelis ate, slept, and breathed the expected battle with Rome. They longed for a military deliverer in the same way the Jews did who lived in Germany and Poland during W.W.II. Can you imagine some "deliverer" coming to the Jews in Germany during that war and trying to convince them that the best way to gain victory was for him to die at the hands of the Germans? Wouldn't they have written him off as a basket case? Wouldn't we?

It was much more difficult for Christ, because it was so obvious to anyone who followed Him for more than a day that He commanded enough power to topple a thousand Roman armies. Jesus faced the seemingly impossible task of acting very much like the Messiah—healing, raising the dead, miraculously feeding thousands—but at the same time doing everything possible to avoid being labeled as such.

So then, every time someone connected Jesus' work with that of the traditional "Messiah," He told them to keep it a secret. As the first part of His strategy, He refused to be connected with that bad meaning of the word. Whenever that label was used He said, "*Shhhhhh*, don't say that again, don't say that to anyone, don't get Me and that word matched up in any way."

In fact, the Savior found a new name for Himself. He threw out the word *Messiah* completely and used a new term, "Son of Man," which came from Daniel 7:13. This became His favorite self-designation because He could inject into it His own meanings and connotations (see Mark 8:30).

Christ focused on reeducating a few people.

The second major part of Jesus' strategy was to focus on reeducating only a few disciples during His ministry rather than a whole nation. It would tax His skill and wisdom to the utmost just to open twelve closed minds in the time available, never mind whole multitudes. These few followers could later teach the meaning of His sufferings to the rest of Israel and then the world. Jesus depended on the disciples "getting it," on their understanding the meaning of His mission and death. The full weight of Christ's hopes now rested on the shoulders of these twelve unsuspecting men.

It is interesting to note that Jesus made His task far more difficult by choosing certain men to be His disciples. Think of Simon the Zealot. The Zealots were bad news. They were fanatical Jewish nationalists, extremists in their desire to overthrow Rome. They eventually developed into what were called the "Sicarii," the Assassins, who devoted themselves to a career of murder and bloodshed. "They received their name from the *sica,* the little curved sword, which they carried below their robes, and which they plunged into the bodies of their enemies at every possible opportunity. The Assassins . . . were terrorists."[2]

The Zealots were similar to the modern-day Hamas among contemporary Palestinians. On the television news we too often hear about members of Hamas maiming and killing Israelis through suicide bombings and gunfire. That is a fairly accurate picture of how Jewish Zealots reacted to Romans in Jesus' day. Such was very likely the fanatical, violent background of Simon the Zealot.

There is also considerable evidence that "Judas the son of James" (see Luke 6:16) belonged to the Zealots as well. Two major historic manuscripts refer to him as "Judas the Zealot."[3]

So why did Jesus choose such men as disciples? One answer is that the Savior knew that selecting people as followers whose lives were headed in the opposite direction of all He stood for would demonstrate the power of the gospel to change selfish hearts. He also knew that such men would make marvelous allies if He could turn their longing to destroy into a longing to love.

There is another miracle tucked away in this story. The Zealots eventually not only hated Rome, they also came to hate any Jew who sympathized or cooperated with Rome in any way, especially tax collectors. The "Mokhes," Jewish customs agents, were the worst of all the tax gatherers, the bottom of the barrel. They collected as much as they could extort from their fellow countrymen on behalf of Rome. They imposed sales tax; bridge tax; harbor tax; road tax; taxes on carts, wheels, axles, animals, river crossings, boats; and on and on.[4] They sucked the populace dry. The Zealots bitterly despised this kind of traitor Jew and dreamed of placing a sharp knife neatly between their ribs.

So what did Jesus do? He chose one of these very tax collectors, Matthew, to be a member of the Twelve. Talk about explosive mixes! Frankly, it is amazing that Simon and Judas didn't take Matthew aside in a back alley one night and kill him!

Jesus also had to contend with the contrary influence of Judas Iscariot, who was one of the main promoters of the "Let's make Jesus King" theme. Judas also frequently instigated the debates among the disciples about who was the greatest.[5]

Christ faced the overwhelming task of completely changing the thinking, attitudes, and values of twelve such fractured misfits and extremists in a very short time. He had to somehow convince them to accept His suffering and death.

One day, after feeding five thousand people and dispatching His disciples across the lake, the Savior went off alone to pray. Ellen White informs us, "It was painful to Jesus that their [the disciples'] conceptions of His kingdom were, to so great a degree, limited to worldly aggrandizement and honor. For them the burden was heavy upon His heart, and He poured out His supplications with bitter agony and tears."[6] The countdown to Calvary continued.

Jesus' first mention of His upcoming sufferings to the disciples did not come until about *nine months before the crucifixion.* Why wait so long? It took that long to build up a trust relationship with the Twelve. Otherwise they would have immediately dismissed Him as hopelessly deluded and left Him for good.

Shortly *before* the Transfiguration Jesus told His disciples pointedly for the first time that He would go into Jerusalem and:

- suffer many things,
- be rejected by the elders, chief priests, and scribes, and
- be killed and rise on the third day (see Matthew 16:21-26; Mark 8:31; Luke 9:22-25).

The timing and context of this first revelation of Christ's upcoming suffering is particularly significant. He waited until just before the Transfiguration because that event clearly demonstrated His power and provided a ringing endorsement from heaven. The presence of Moses and Elijah also provided a compelling confirmation of His teachings. On the Mount, God the Father added His own stirring admonition to the disciples, " 'Listen to Him,' " in an attempt to get them to pay attention to Jesus' description of His upcoming pain (Mark 9:7).

It is interesting to note that when Peter rebuked Jesus for talking about His death, Christ reacted vehemently by saying, " 'Get behind me, Satan! You are a hindrance to me; for you are not on the side of God, but of men' " (Matthew 16:23). Why such an intense reaction? Peter had unknowingly hit a raw nerve within the heart of Christ. The apostle didn't understand how mercilessly the devil had hounded Jesus throughout His life with the special temptation to turn aside from the Cross and all the terrible sufferings involved.

Shortly *after* the Transfiguration Jesus again revealed that He would:

- be betrayed into the hands of men, and
- be killed and rise the third day (see Matthew 17:22, 23; Mark 9:31; Luke 9:43-45).

Jesus couldn't have made it clearer! Sadly we read in the book of Mark,

"But they did not understand the saying, and they were afraid to ask him" (Mark (9:32). The disciples chose not to discuss Christ's description of His not too distant torture.

Certain topics are just too unthinkable for some people to talk about. Early in World War II, many Jews refused to believe reports that the Nazis were slaughtering entire families by the thousands. The image was too horrific to accept, or even discuss. So it was with the disciples in relation to the sufferings of Christ. The very thought that the Messiah would die was so unimaginable that they rejected the idea as utterly ridiculous.

Amazingly, it was only a short time later that the disciples debated who would be the greatest in the kingdom after the Romans were overthrown (see Mark 9:33-34). Ellen White comments, "To the heart of Christ it was a bitter task to press His way against the fears, disappointment, and unbelief of His beloved disciples."[7]

With just *a few more months* to go before His death, Jesus again referred to the fact that He would perish in Jerusalem (see Luke 13:23).

How Jesus must have agonized to find a way to make Himself understood! It was now March or early April of the year of His death, A.D. 31. There were, at most, only weeks left before Calvary! In Luke 17:25 the Savior explained that He must suffer and be rejected, but it fell on deaf ears. Christ then took the disciples aside and again tried desperately to compel them to understand what lay ahead. With a great sense of urgency, He outlined His sufferings in amazing detail, telling the disciples that He would go to Jerusalem and be:

- betrayed to the chief priests and scribes,
- condemned to death and delivered to the Gentiles,
- mocked, spitefully treated, scourged and spit on,
- crucified and then rise the third day (see Matthew 20:18, 19; Mark 10:32-34; Luke 18:31-34).

Jesus shared these heartbreaking words in the context of the raising of Lazarus in order to let the disciples know that He could conquer death, even His own death. Incredibly, it was right after this soul-stirring preview of Jesus' agony that James and John came and asked for the top positions in His kingdom when He conquered Rome! How cruel of them to take the words that Jesus shared, painful words that were so carefully chosen, and simply ignore them as so much unimportant mumbling. Shortly after this incident Jesus healed two blind men as a living illustration of the need for the disciples to have their own eyes opened (see Matthew 20:29-34).

Time continued to tick away. On the day before the Last Supper, Jesus plainly stated, "You know that after two days the Passover is coming, and the Son of Man will be delivered up to be crucified" (Matthew 26:2, RSV). Again no response.

There were now only a few pitifully short hours between Christ and the cross. Calvary loomed up before Him. He took His disciples to the Upper Room a final time and chose to act out the principles of His kingdom. He resorted to using visual aids to get His message across, just as you would employ with little children. He donned a towel, took a basin of water, and washed twelve pairs of filthy feet. His actions were designed to smash the idea that He came to be an earthly Conqueror. He was, instead, a Servant. Jesus then took bread and the fruit of the vine and said with great earnestness, "Listen, this is my blood which is shed. This is my body that is broken. I am going to die!" The disciples were impressed but still very far from understanding.

The prospect of His sufferings and death being totally misunderstood now seemed inevitable! What heartrending grief the Savior must have felt at the awful thought that no one understood. If I were Jesus, with so much at stake, I would have thrown up my hands and quit trying. But Christ was so incredibly patient and persistent that, despite the lateness of the hour, *He still had a plan. He would try to open their minds by taking them with Him to Gethsemane.*

That night, He left eight of His followers at the entrance to the garden while the other three, Peter, James, and John, went with Him into the inner recesses. These three had witnessed His greatest miracles and had been the recipients of His most careful attention. Any final hope of anyone understanding why He was about to suffer and die now rested squarely on His three closest associates.

In the garden, Jesus deliberately placed Peter, James, and John within earshot, only a stone's throw away from one of His familiar places of prayer. In a few minutes He would undergo the most terrifying experience of His life. Every weapon of hell would be loosed as the sins of the world were laid upon Him and His own heavenly Father forsook Him. And Jesus wanted these three to hear it all. That was one of the primary purposes of His agony in Gethsemane, *to give these three one last opportunity to understand.*

We are told, "He took them with Him . . . that the events they should witness that night, and the lessons of instruction they should receive, might be indelibly printed upon their memories. This was necessary that they might be strengthened for the test just before them."[8] "Had the disciples watched with Christ in His agony, they would have been prepared to behold His suffering upon the cross. They would have *understood* in some degree the nature of his overpowering anguish. . . . Amid the gloom of the most trying hour [the cross], some rays of hope would have lighted up the darkness and *sustained their faith.*"[9]

He carefully admonished them to stay awake and pray. "Please, please, it is tremendously important that you stay alert and listen! Let my pain burn through your misconceptions!" He urged.

An hour passed, and He staggered back to the disciples, His countenance deeply etched with pain and stained with blood. And all three were sleeping. *Sleeping!* (See Matthew 26:36-41.) They had also slept on the Mount of Transfiguration. Again Christ pleaded with them to stay awake, hoping that as they heard His cries of anguish they would be forced to think, forced to understand.

A little later He returned, found them sleeping a second time, and urged them with inexpressible earnestness to remain alert. In a little while, sleep overwhelmed them a final time, and though His disappointment was immense, He simply commented, " 'The spirit indeed is willing, but the flesh is weak' " (Matthew 26:42-46, KJV).

Here is the gospel! With so much at stake, under such extreme pressure, in the face of such an appalling display of human weakness, Jesus' love for His followers did not waiver. I would have exploded, "You dummies! You're all a bunch of losers!" But Christ did not condemn, He only sought to uplift and encourage! He simply said, "The spirit is willing, but oh that flesh!"

The Son of God must now go to torture and death realizing that not one person in the entire world knows why. How futile it all must have appeared!

At one point Mary Magdalene had perceived that He would die, but the disciples later disabused her of that "foolish" notion. She had planned to anoint Him for burial. "But now many were declaring that He was about to be crowned king. Her grief was turned to joy, and she was eager to be first in honoring her Lord."[10] Later, as Christ hung on the cross, the response of the thief indicated that at least he understood somewhat, but this enlightened robber would soon be dead and could explain nothing.

So pervasive and all encompassing was the conspiracy of misunderstanding that the Jews wrongly interpreted even the one sentence that was the crux of the entire plan of salvation. Jesus cried, " 'Eloi, Eloi, Lama Sabachthani' " (My God, My God, why hast Thou forsaken Me?) and the Jews thought He was deliriously calling for Elijah.

The final crushing blow came when the only One who did understand, the only One who did appreciate His sacrifice, His heavenly Father, totally forsook Him on the cross.

On Golgotha there was absolutely nothing to indicate to Christ that His death would ever be seen as anything more than a fitting end to a deluded misadventure. All the evidence shouted out that, at best, His death would simply be remembered for a few short years as the unfair execution of a very good Man.

1. Matt Sumner, "Cuban Missile Crisis," available on the Internet at http://nutmeg.ctstateu.edu/depts/edu/textbooks/cuban.html
2. William Barclay, *The Master's Men* (New York: Abingdon Press, 1959), 96.
3. Ibid., 118.
4. Ibid., 61.
5. *The Desire of Ages*, 718, 719.
6. Ibid., 379.
7. Ibid., 486.
8. Ellen G. White, *The Sufferings of Christ* (Hagerstown, Md.: Review and Herald, n.d.), 16, 17.
9. *The Desire of Ages*, 714. Italics supplied.
10. Ibid., 559.

Chapter 4

Physical Torture

"Dad, what is that long, jagged scar on your knee, and why do you sometimes walk with a limp?" For many years my father changed the subject when I asked that question. Recently, however, he let his mind drift back to World War II, and the story tumbled out.

Traveling across France in a troop train, he sat in one of the officers' cars up front. Sabotage sent the train careening down an unfinished sidetrack. In the next few horrendous moments, several passenger cars accordioned together, demolishing everything in sight and crushing my dad's legs beneath debris. Only ten of the thirty officers in his car survived. Doctors told him he'd never walk again. The more I learned about his injuries and courageous rehabilitation, the more I admired him.

It is natural to be deeply concerned about the sufferings of those we love. And if I care about my dad's scars, how much more should I care about the scars of my Lord?

Our best Friend and Savior has His own painful story to tell if we care enough to inquire and to listen. "Jesus, where did You get those awful wounds in your hands and feet? And that injury to your side, how did that happen?"

I am not fond of the subject of physical pain. But it is impossible to fully appreciate Jesus' sacrifice without dealing directly with His bodily torments.

No shortcuts, no sweeping under the rug, no averting the eyes, no exaggerating for effect or glorifying gore, but no sanitizing either. The devil would love to have us gloss over the details. The better we understand the torture, the better we understand who Satan really is and the more deeply we appreciate what Christ endured on our behalf.

For my wife, pain is defined by childbirth. "For crying out loud, someone give me something! Knock me out . . . I've had it!" For me, pain is a kidney test gone awry. The doctor inadvertently used too much dye, causing my kidneys to swell up to the size of Delaware. When the anesthetic wore off at home, I sank to my knees in misery, clawing at the edge of the bed. I waited there forever while my wife bought a prescription painkiller at the drugstore. All of that pales to insignificance, however, when compared to what Christ experienced from shortly after midnight to 3:00 P.M. on a fateful Friday in A.D. 31.

The Gospel writers didn't go into a lot of detail about Jesus' trials and crucifixion because they didn't need to. Those scenes were as familiar to people then as terrorist bombings are to us today. Frequently the people were eyewitnesses to the kind of cruelty Christ suffered. We are at a comfortable distance, a Laodicean distance, from those scenes and need to be reminded.

At the very outset we must clear up a common, but crucial, misunderstanding. Many people believe that Satan's purpose was to kill Christ through crucifixion. Not really. The evil one's plan was more complex and clever than that.

The trials and Crucifixion were actually part of an overall strategy Satan devised long before Calvary. His plan included four amazingly potent temptations, each one more severe than the one before it, to be used during Christ's public ministry. They differed in approach but had a common goal—*to get Jesus to use His divine power in His own behalf or to step outside the plan of salvation in some way.*

The first three temptations were unsheathed in rapid-fire succession in the wilderness, and the evil one was absolutely dumbfounded when they failed. There was only one temptation left more powerful than these, a temptation the devil hoped he would never have to use. Jesus' victory in the wilderness, however, left Satan with no alternative. *The devil planned to torture Christ into giving up or sinning.* There was grave danger here for the devil himself, however. The greater the torture, the greater the possibility that Christ would die. Satan knew the Scriptures well and understood that if he pushed too far and actually killed Christ, he himself would be unveiled before the watching universe as a murderer and thus ensure his own ultimate destruction. Nonetheless, in desperation, the evil one chose to implement this extremely potent, yet risky, plan.

To achieve his purpose, Satan utilized the most horrific form of torture then available—crucifixion. The whole process of condemning someone to the cross, with its abusive trials and excruciating scourge, was designed to inflict extraordinary, prolonged pain. Satan intended to heap so much physical and mental suffering on Christ during the trials that He would retaliate or refuse to go on before He ever got near Golgotha. And if by some impossible chance the Savior did reach Calvary without sinning, crucifixion itself was so cruel and overwhelming that Jesus would surely falter spiritually.

The Spirit of Prophecy summarizes the devil's purpose. "The chief priests and elders were inspired by [Satan and his angels] to insult and abuse Jesus in a manner the most difficult for human nature to bear. Satan hoped that such mockery and violence would call forth from the Son of God some complaint or murmur; or that He would manifest His divine power and wrench Himself from the grasp of the multitude, *and that thus the plan of salvation might at last fail.*"[1]

And we must always keep clearly in mind that "suffering was more keenly felt by [Christ]; for His spiritual nature was free from every taint of sin. Therefore His desire for the removal of suffering was stronger than human beings can experience."[2]

Jesus was protected from physical harm by guardian angels for the three and a half years of His public ministry. But Satan knew the prophecies and knew when the Son of God would be given fully into his hands, and he anticipated that awesome final encounter with nervous delight.

"Now the tempter had come for the last fearful struggle. For this he had been preparing during the three years of Christ's ministry. Everything was at stake with him. If he failed here, his hope of mastery was lost; the kingdoms of the world would finally become Christ's; he himself would be overthrown and cast out. But if Christ could be overcome, the earth would become Satan's kingdom, and the human race would be forever in his power."[3]

After Christ was seized by the mob in Gethsemane, the sequence of events was as follows:

- Interrogated by Annas (ex-high priest)
- Interrogated by Annas and Caiaphas
- Night trial before the Sanhedrin (not full session)
- *Taken to guardroom and beaten by mob*
- Day trial before the full Sanhedrin
- *Priests and mob beat Christ*
- First trial before Pilate

- Trial before Herod
- *Herod, mob, and soldiers beat Christ*
- Second trial before Pilate
- Scourged in view of multitude
- *Soldiers mock and beat Christ in Praetorium*
- Scourged a second time
- Crucified

From this list it is evident that Christ was *beaten* four *separate times*, quite apart from the scourgings with a whip. Satan's primary focus was, in fact, on the trials themselves.

The first beating

The initial beating took place *after the first Sanhedrin trial*, around 4:00 A.M. Christ was bound and escorted by guards through the large, open courtyard of the high priest's palace. He gladly sucked in large drafts of crisp, refreshing night air that was cool against His sweat-drenched skin and robe.

The soldiers had to shove their way through a large unruly crowd that had gathered for a glimpse of the hated prisoner. Torches cast an eerie, flickering yellow light on hundreds of angry faces as accusations, ridicule, and obscenities rained down. Christ was hurried along and deposited in a nearby jail cell to await the second Jewish trial at dawn. The small, cold, musty cell reeked of rancid sweat and waste. A guard gripped Jesus' shoulder and shoved Him down onto a crude rough-hewn bench set against the rock wall. Christ closed His eyes and let His head slump forward onto His chest in exhaustion. His mind reeled as He recounted the momentous events of the evening and offered a prayer for strength to endure.

Remarkably, the temple police then left the cell open, stepped aside, and gave the bloodthirsty multitude complete access to Christ, with the frightening freedom to do with Him as they pleased.

"Then they spat in His face, and struck Him with their fists; and some slapped Him in the face, . . . saying, 'Prophesy to us, You Christ, the Messiah! Who was it that struck You?' " (Matthew 26:67, 68, Amplified).

The Spirit of Prophecy informs us that the rabble "took license to manifest all the satanic elements of their nature. Christ's very nobility and godlike bearing goaded them to *madness*."[4] "His persecutors, having Him completely in their power, try to do Him as much harm as possible in mind and body alike."[5]

After a deep, rasping gargle, many filed forward to spit out thick, stinking

49

mucous onto Jesus' hair, face, and beard (see Matthew 26:67). In the Middle Eastern culture of that time, spitting on someone was a vulgar expression of the utmost disdain and contempt. Then came the onslaught of fists and punches. Luke adds that at one point the temple police themselves actually joined in the abuse. "Now the men who were holding Jesus mocked him and beat him" (Luke 22:63, RSV). The Greek word for "beat" in this verse indicates a blow of "great violence."[6]

"Hey, get me that old robe over there!" someone yelled. "Let's see if this fool is for real." They threw a frayed, stained, coarse garment over Jesus' head so He could no longer see. Laughter rang out as ruffians passed by the Son of God, taking turns slapping Him hard on the side of the head. After each hit they chided, " 'Prophesy! Who is it that struck you?' " (Luke 22:64, RSV; see also Mark 14:65).

They were playing a brutal form of a well-known child's game of that day, similar to our Blind Man's Bluff, making a mockery of His role as prophet.[7] There was no way the Savior could anticipate the blows and avert the impact. His head snapped back with each roundhouse, open-fisted assault. The Spirit of Prophecy indicates that heavenly beings were so outraged that they had to be held back from intervening. *"There was commotion among the angels*. They would have rescued Him instantly, but their commanding angels restrained them."[8]

When the fire-storm finally abated, Christ slumped forward, eyes swollen, lips battered, cheeks deeply bruised, blood pouring from His nose and oozing from a variety of cuts about His head. He coughed repeatedly and spat up red-tinged saliva. Ellen White sums up the scene with the chilling comment, "Never was criminal treated in so inhuman a manner as was the Son of God."[9]

The second beating

Immediately after the second Sanhedrin trial, sometime between 5:00 and 6:00 A.M., the Jewish leaders again vented their pent-up frustration by allowing the gathered crowd to attack the Savior, this time within the Jewish judgment hall itself. The people rushed upon Christ with a sudden wave of unnerving shouts and curses.

The Spirit of Prophecy makes the startling statement that this scene of abuse and mockery was "worse even than that received from the ignorant rabble" earlier, in the jail cell.[10] "Had it not been for the Roman soldiers, Jesus would not have lived to be nailed to the cross of Calvary."[11] The soldiers themselves, who regularly witnessed scenes of stomach-churning cruelty, were angry at the brutal way Christ was treated.[12]

The third beating

Aging Herod Antipas, tetrarch of Syria, was visiting Jerusalem during Passover to gain political brownie points with the masses. This was the same erratic, immoral leader who sliced off John the Baptist's holy head. Jesus warily called him "that fox" (Luke 13:32).

Christ arrived in Herod's court "special delivery" from a bewildered Pontius Pilate. Herod treated Jesus as a curiosity, an amusing wonderworker. He plied Jesus with questions and eager requests for miracles but was met with stony silence and ignored. The volatile king's irritation quickly escalated to fury, and his mock trial deteriorated to another scene of terrible abuse. "And Herod with his soldiers treated him with contempt and mocked him" (Luke 23:11).

"Like wild beasts, the crowd darted upon their prey. *Jesus was dragged this way and that.* . . . Had not the Roman soldiers interposed, and forced back the maddened throng, the Savior would have been torn in pieces."[13] A bright robe was thrown over Christ's shoulders, and people came forward in mock worship of the ridiculed king, spitting on him in contempt. We are given the poignant and touching observation that at one point Jesus "meekly raised His hand and wiped [the spittle] off."[14]

Shuddering at the violence of His enemies and the enormity of His pain, the Lamb of God was goaded the 600 feet back to Pilate's judgment hall. We are told that Christ was now "tottering with weariness, pale and wounded."[15] In fact, when the Son of God arrived back at Pilate's trial, He fell from exhaustion upon the marble pavement.[16] The extent of Christ's injuries at this point from the three beatings can be imagined by Ellen White's vivid description of Him as being "covered with wounds."[17]

The fourth beating

While the cross and nails were being sought, the Roman soldiers brought Christ to the barracks area in the Praetorium to mock the idea of Him being a Jewish king. This beating was not terribly severe but certainly quite hurtful and harmful nonetheless.

After removing Jesus' own robe, they replaced it with a scarlet military cloak to simulate the garments of a ruler (see Matthew 27:28). A crown of sharp thorny vines was ceremoniously pressed onto Jesus' head and a reed scepter placed in His hand. Someone snatched the reed and hit the crown, causing blood to flow from several puncture wounds in Jesus' scalp. Others took up the idea, dancing in turns around the Son of God and pounding in the thorns until blood "[flowed] down His face and beard."[18] The galaxy-Maker's cheeks, chin, ears, neck, and shoulders were soon covered with numerous rivulets of glistening crimson.

Others leaned over and spat on the Son of God in contempt until a disgusting mixture of blood, sweat, and spittle soaked His hair and beard. The apostle John significantly ratchets up the cruelty of the scene by telling us that soldiers repeatedly filed by and slapped Christ harshly across the face[19] (see John 19:2, 3). "They marred that face with blows and cruelty."[20]

Scourging

In addition to the four beatings, Jesus also endured the horror of the dreaded Roman scourge. The devil dramatically tightened the screws of suffering as Jesus was forced to endure scourging an unheard-of *two separate times*. "From insult to renewed insult, from mockery to mockery, twice tortured by the scourge,— all that night there had been scene after scene of a character to try the soul of man to the uttermost."[21]

The first scourging incident occurred partway through the trial before Pilate. Luke recounts the scene as the Roman governor announced, " 'I will therefore chastise him and release him' " (Luke 23:16). Pilate hoped the Jews would agree to a kind of plea bargain and content themselves with giving Christ the lash rather than the cross. *The second scourging* occurred later, after Pilate had pronounced the death sentence: "Then he released for them Barabbas, and having scourged Jesus, delivered him to be crucified" (Matthew 27:26).

The scourge itself "was a multi-thonged, short-handled whip made of ox leather, knotted with small knuckle-bones, or lead balls, or even bronze hooks made to tear the flesh. [The victim] would be . . . hung by his hands from rings in the ceiling, or against a wall, or spread-eagled around a pillar, and then, thus exposed and vulnerable, he would be flogged back and front by two or more men, chosen for their physical strength, and trained to inflict the most frightful injuries without actually killing."[22]

Virchel E. Wood has also commented that "hemorrhage was intense and the skin and flesh became lacerated to ribbons."[23]

Some have questioned how anyone, even the Savior, could possibly have survived a double scourging. There are actually different underlying Greek words the Gospel writers used to describe what Christ endured. They range in meaning from a severe *whipping* to the flesh-destroying *scourging* described above. It may be that Christ was initially whipped and only later given the full, nightmarish scourge. The Romans did not have any prescribed number of blows, so it may also be that they scourged Jesus in both instances but one beating was much more severe than the other. In any case, the Son of God was horribly torn and bruised.

We can try to imagine the scene as, just prior to being marched off to Calvary, He was lacerated for the second time:

The Savior's hands were untied. A tall, attractive, weathered soldier with a closely cropped, dark brown beard removed Jesus' belt, yanked the outer robe away, and removed the seamless inner garment by pulling it up over Christ's head. Jesus' arms were stretched around a thick granite column and tied at the wrists, drawing His body up closely against the smooth, cool stone. Jesus' sweaty skin glistened in the reflected light. The muscles were well-defined and firm.

At a signal, two coarse-looking veteran soldiers swaggered forward. The sharp crack of leather thongs echoed through the hall. The troopers positioned themselves, one on each side of Jesus, bringing the scourges to rest at their sides, pausing to heighten the victim's inner terror. The Savior's lips were pursed, the mouth drawn up. He glanced down at the implements of misery and then closed His eyes tightly, bracing for the initial blow. The soldiers took pride in how quickly they could make the victim's knees buckle, how soon they could cause blood to flow down the torso and out along the grooves between the large granite blocks.

The soldier on the left drew his scourge back behind his head and held it there momentarily. They would take turns in a well-practiced, coordinated attack on the victim's skin, muscles, tendons, nerves, and blood vessels. (Their work reminded some of the skilled movements of a butcher). The scourge was brought down with great force as the soldier took a step forward and threw his entire weight into the stroke. The iron balls tied along the leather at various intervals smacked into the Savior's shoulder blades and the bony protrusions of the spinal cord, causing His body to involuntarily shudder and then flex inward as if trying to curl up in a fetal position. The hooks dug deeply into Jesus' back, then ripped and tore, gouging out pieces of skin and muscle as the scourge was yanked back for another callous blow. Christ moaned in pain. Already blood streamed down. That was *one* stroke. The first few blows would put you in the emergency room for stitches. By twenty or thirty you would need to be in intensive care. Many died before the final lash.

"A number of the Jews of Alexandria who were scourged on the order of the [prefect], Flaccus, died during the punishment, and the rest only recovered after a long period of disablement. Josephus records that he himself had some of his opponents in Galilean Tarícheæ scourged until their entrails were visible."[24]

"The severe scourging, with its intense pain and appreciable blood loss, most probably left Jesus in a preshock state. . . . Therefore, even before the actual crucifixion, Jesus' physical condition was at least serious and possibly critical."[25] The cumulative effect of the various torments during those early hours of Friday certainly took their miserable toll.

Crucifixion

The soldiers now hurriedly made preparation for Christ to suffer the death reserved for insurrectionists, slaves, and the vilest of criminals. The Romans adopted crucifixion from other cultures and perfected it through extensive use as an exquisite, slow torture, producing maximum pain and suffering.

"In the Roman provinces crucifixion was one of the most important means of maintaining order and security, and the history of the turbulent province of Judea in particular contains numerous accounts of crucifixions. . . . During the siege of Jerusalem [A.D. 70] five hundred or more Jewish prisoners were crucified daily in every possible position in front of the town, until at last wood for the crosses, and space in which to set them up, ran short."[26]

Our English word *excruciating* appropriately comes from a Latin word meaning "out of the cross."[27] It is true that Jesus' spiritual suffering under the weight of our sins became so intense on the cross that "His physical pain was hardly felt."[28] But that was the case primarily from noon to 3:00 P.M. Until then, He felt every dreadful ounce of physical torture the devil heaped upon Him.

The crossbar, weighing 75 to 125 pounds, was laid on the Savior's bruised and battered shoulders. He could barely walk, and He staggered only a very few yards toward Calvary before the heavy load crumpled Him to the ground. Because His arms were tied to the wood, He could not reach out and break His fall. His head hit the gravel first, then His shoulder and knees, scraping Him badly. Whipped to His feet, He courageously stumbled a few more feet, then swayed, tried to catch His balance, reeled to one side, and crumpled to the ground a final time. The professional soldiers, who saw death daily, leaned down to examine His condition and initially pronounced Him dead.[29] He eventually revived, but extensive loss of blood and unrelenting trauma rendered Him incapable of carrying the load. Simon of Cyrene was commandeered, and the mournful procession lumbered on. It would not be hard to retrace the Savior's journey later, because "*at every step* was left blood which flowed from [Christ's] wounds."[30]

At the place of crucifixion, Christ was stripped entirely naked. (For comparison, imagine yourself being displayed nude for six hours in downtown New York City during the height of Christmas shopping.) The soldiers shoved Him to the ground, positioned His arms on the cross, and drove a three-eighths-inch iron spike through each wrist. The damage to the median nerve would send regular, fiery bolts of pain shooting up His arms for hours. The feet were positioned and either nailed separately to each side of the upright or the legs were turned to one side with the feet nailed on top of each other through the heel.

The thieves resisted and struggled, filling the air with curses and screams of agony. Christ meekly submitted without crying out, but He was bathed in sweat, and His body involuntarily convulsed and shuddered after each hammer blow. It was while the nails were being driven in that He looked heavenward and uttered the prayer of forgiveness: " 'Father, forgive them [whack]; for they [whack] know not what they do' "[31] (Luke 23:34).

Jesus gritted His teeth and glanced around wide-eyed as He felt Himself and His cross being rudely lifted upward by several careless soldiers then suddenly thrust violently downward into position. As the end of the upright hit the bottom of the drilled hole with a body-jolting thud, the wounds in His wrists gaped open, tearing flesh and causing a fierce spasm of pain. Blood continued to flow from the four beatings, from each area of flesh mangled by the scourge, from each puncture wound made by the thorns, and from the injuries created by the nails. Frankly, Christ was a bloody mess. Flies gathered, crawling and picking at the many wounds. The scene was nothing at all like the sanitized crucifixion paintings of the Middle Ages.

One of the perks of the soldier's job was the right to keep the clothing of the condemned, a kind of potluck system for adding to one's wardrobe. All of Christ's clothes lay in a disheveled, bloodstained heap about six yards from His cross. After nailing the Son of God and stabilizing the upright, the guards sat down together to divvy up the goods. There were four soldiers attending Christ and five pieces of clothing, which presented a sticky problem in distribution.

"The last three crucifixions I didn't get anything worth spit. It's about time I got something decent, like this inner robe right here." The seasoned soldier held it up for closer examination. "Too bad its got so much blood all over it. Won't be easy cleaning this thing up."

"Leave that alone. Let's deal with this other stuff first," the officer in charge admonished. "Who wants the headgear? How about the belt and shoes?"

When they tried to select a new owner for the seamless robe, it caused such harsh bickering that the matter had to be decided by the casting of lots[32] (see John 19:23, 24).

The soldiers eventually settled in for the boring vigil, dug out their lunches, and gulped some cheap, homemade wine. Suddenly one of them slapped his knee and shouted, "Hey, we're being terrible hosts, boys. Havin' our own little party down here and leavin' out our royal visitor, the king. We should show more respect."

The soldier rose, walked up directly in front of Christ, and held out his wine cup in a toast (see Luke 23:36, 37). "To you, sir. To your genius, your visionary leadership, your . . . your brief but brilliant reign. Here, would you like some wine? Reach out and take it. It's right here. What's the matter?" He jiggled the cup about three or four feet from Jesus' face for a few seconds, smiled, then said sarcastically, "Time's up," and flung the contents onto the ground.

The crowd again joined the mockery. "If you're King of the Jews, come down off that cross and let's see if your God really is more powerful than Rome." It was, in fact, the voice of Satan, making one last, desperate attempt to get the Savior to abandon heaven's plan.

As He hung between heaven and earth, the Lord of the universe felt

> The pain of the nails, and the severed nerves grating on them;
> The pain of cramps, with no relief;
> The pain of extension, drawn out and agonizing;
> The pain of slow suffocation, the struggle for air;
> The pain in the blood, in the heart, in the head;
> The pain in the legs and feet, the standing on pain;
> The pain of the wood of the cross against the flayed flesh of the back, . . .
> The pain of thirst, the pain of fever, with no relief;
> And the pain of sin, with no relief, with no relief.[33]

In order to take in a sufficient amount of air to speak, Christ had to press down on His feet and raise His body upward, relieving the constriction of the solar plexus. As a result, He communicated with great difficulty, in short phrases. The harsh Middle Eastern sun continued to bake its three dehydrated victims. At one point Jesus' eyes beckoned the soldiers nearby while His tongue searched for moisture to form the words "I thirst."

Eternity was compressed into six hours on a hill where children were not allowed to play, where strangers were warned not to wander, where things were done that families spent decades trying to forget. Jesus' life forces were nearly spent. With His last ounce of strength, He pressed upward painfully on the nails one more time, looked out toward the hills, and shouted " 'It is finished' "; then He bowed His head and died.

"O God, who said, Let there be light: and there was light; and whose Son is the true Light, which lighteth every man that cometh into the world: give us light now that we may see Thy Son, and seeing Him, grow more like Him."[34]

1. Ellen G. White, *The Story of Redemption* (Hagerstown, Md.: Review and Herald, 1947), 213.
2. Ellen G. White, *Seventh-day Adventist Bible Commentary* (Hagerstown, Md.: Review and Herald, 1957), 7-A:224.
3. *The Desire of Ages*, 686, 687.
4. Ibid., 710, italics supplied.
5. Norval Geldenhuys, *Commentary on the Gospel of Luke: The International Commentary on the New Testament*, 586.
6. *Vine's Expository Dictionary of the New Testament* (New York, N.Y.: Thomas Nelson, 1985), 54.
7. Raymond E. Brown, *The Death of the Messiah* (New York, N.Y.: Doubleday, 1994), 1:574, 575.
8. *The Story of Redemption*, 215, italics supplied.
9. *The Desire of Ages*, 710.
10. Ibid., 714.
11. Ibid., 715.
12. Ibid.
13. Ibid., 731.
14. Arthur L. White, *Ellen G. White: The Australian Years 1891-1900* (Hagerstown, Md.: Review and Herald, 1983), 4:386.
15. Ellen G. White, *Signs of the Times®*, 31 Jan. 1900.
16. See Ellen G. White, *Redemption, or the Sufferings of Christ, His Trial, and Crucifixion*, The Redemption Series no. 5 (Battle Creek, Mich: Seventh-day Adventist Publishing Association, 1877-1878), 61.
17. *The Desire of Ages*, 734.
18. Ibid.
19. Raymond E. Brown, *The Death of the Messiah* (New York, N.Y.: Doubleday, 1994), 1:868; Leon Morris, *The Gospel According to John* (Grand Rapids, Mich.: Eerdmans, 1971), 791.
20. Ellen G. White, *Spiritual Gifts* (Hagerstown, Md.: Review and Herald, 1944), 1:61.
21. *The Desire of Ages*, 742.
22. G. W. Target, *Watch With Me* (London: Gerald Duckworth, 1961), 89.
23. Virchel E. Wood, *Adventist Review*, 31 Mar. 1983.
24. Josef Blinzler, *The Trial of Jesus* (Westminster, Md.: Newman Press, 1959), 223.
25. William D. Edwards, Wesley J. Gabel, Floyd E. Hosmer, "On the Physical Death of Jesus Christ," *JAMA*, Mar. 21, 1986, 1458.
26. Josef Blinzler, *The Trial of Jesus*, 246, 247.
27. Edwards, Gabel, and Hosmer, "On the Physical Death of Jesus Christ," 1461.
28. *The Desire of Ages*, 753.
29. See *The Story of Redemption*, 220, 221.

30. *The Sufferings of Christ*, 33.
31. See *The Story of Redemption*, 222.
32. *The Desire of Ages*, 746, 751.
33. Target, *Watch With Me*, 94.
34. Ibid., 94, 95.

Chapter 5

The News

Many people today can tell you exactly where they were when they heard about President Kennedy's assassination. Likewise, countless Jews and Gentiles could easily recount the moment they heard the news of Christ's arrest. People became aware of Jesus' fate at different times and in different ways. *We might imagine several possible scenarios, such as the ones listed below.*

Labbaeus and Anna

Jesus' followers awakened to a nightmarish scene in the Garden of Gethsemane. Shock and anger took over the disciples' hearts as the Jewish leaders and the callous mob arrested Christ. Filled with terror, Peter proposed that they save their own necks and make a run for it under the camouflage of night. Peter and John followed their Lord at a reasonably safe distance. The other disciples might have nervously knocked on the doors of certain trusted friends, casting sidelong glances into the moonlit night, trying to catch the earliest possible reflection of Roman swords.

Perhaps Matthew took refuge at the home of a fellow publican, Labbaeus, who became a Christian through Matthew's witness. Sometime between midnight and 1:00 A.M. Labbaeus and his wife, Anna, were jarred awake by insistent rapping.

"Who is it?" he inquired, his voice cautious and raspy from the sudden disruption of sleep.

"Matthew. It's me, Matthew. Let me in. Hurry!" Labbaeus pushed aside the bolt; the door creaked slightly as he opened it, and the former tax collector quickly slipped inside the small candle-lit room. Extremely agitated, Matthew paced randomly. He ached with self-recrimination and shivered with fear. Anna threw a blanket over his shoulders and offered hot broth. She and her husband were stunned at Matthew's recital of recent events as he shared pieces of the terrible story in a hurried, disjointed manner.

"In the Garden . . . we were sleeping. Then the awful shouting and arrest. They tied Christ and took Him away! Judas himself led the mob. Judas! Can you believe that traitor actually led them right to us? Those stinkin', conniving priests. I should have suspected. Roman guards came with swords and clubs. We were lucky to get out of there with our lives, I tell you! I don't know what's happened to Jesus since. We could all be killed. I just don't know." They decided to wait through the night and listen for trouble.

Early in the morning the group felt compelled to wend their way toward the city, heads covered, to make inquiries of friends. They neared Jerusalem and hesitated at a final bend in the road. An oncoming contingent of Roman soldiers sent them scurrying behind a low, vine-covered stone wall. Upon entering the old city, their attention was drawn to what seemed like rhythmic chanting coming from the direction of Pilate's headquarters. Suddenly a crowd spilled into the open area outside the northern gate, screaming, "Death to the traitor! Crucify the Gentile lover!" At a considerable distance they followed the multitudes that accompanied Jesus along the bloody, heart-stopping climb to Golgotha.[1]

Jason

The streets of Jerusalem never slept. Prostitutes, thieves, and urchins of the night all formed an unsavory alliance of illegal underground activity. The Romans treated this uneducated, lawless element of society as dogs react to fleas. Festivals such as Passover provided unparalleled opportunities for mischief and dishonest profit. On such occasions the shady ranks of delinquents swelled immeasurably, and many of these unscrupulous people composed the mob that arrested Christ.

One of the veteran night people, Jason, made a meager living as a pickpocket. Short, with a scrubby, graying beard and slight limp, he called out excitedly to some cohorts, "Hey, the soldiers are headed to Gethsemane. I heard they're goin' after that eccentric Galilean! That fool is out of his devil-possessed mind."

Jason hurried to join the gathering mob and elbowed his way to the front, just behind the double rank of uniformed police. He tried to make conversation with the soldiers as the crowd crossed the Kidron Valley. "Tense situation, huh? Sure do appreciate you guys keepin' things safe. Bet you get tired of messin' with jokers like this phony Messiah guy, huh? Real troublemaker, isn't He? Hate these jerks!" He jabbered on in an annoying monologue. As they neared the garden, Jason felt his heart race. He labored to keep up.

He saw Christ apprehended and bound. Like the rest of the mob, the miraculous intervention of the angel and the brilliance of the heavenly light dampened Jason's enthusiasm only slightly. Once Jesus was securely in custody, Jason shouted, "You guys really do great work, you know, never miss a beat." He danced back down the Mount of Olives, eagerly anticipating upcoming events.

Salma

Recently healed of blindness by Christ, Salma heard the news from his daughter as she returned from gathering water about 7:30 A.M. He had just finished putting away the bedclothes when she burst through the door yelling, "Father, they've arrested Him!"

"Who, daughter? Slow down. Who?"

"Jesus! The Romans are putting Him on trial! Janna just said."

Salma checked with neighbors and confirmed the awful rumor. He instructed his wife and daughter to remain home while he sought more information about the Man who was more precious to them than life itself. He soon stepped within the city of Jerusalem and there, at the Praetorium, saw something he never imagined his re-created eyes would ever behold. In the distance he could make out Jesus, on display, bleeding from head to toe. Dismayed at the hatred of the frenzied mob, Salma ran toward the scene, shouting "No! No! You must let Him go, you must! He's innocent!"

A Roman soldier caught him tightly by the arm, jerked him up short, and inquired firmly, "What is that you were sayin'?"

Startled into silence, Salma looked up into the soldier's stern, pockmarked face and stammered simply, "I mean no trouble."

"See that you don't!" was the hard-edged reply.

The sounds of violence filled the air. Salma's heart pounded as the awful cry "Crucify Him, crucify Him" intruded upon the bright, sun-splashed morning.

The orphan

A little orphan boy, whom Jesus had told to throw away his crutches more than a year before, observed the noisy procession from inside the run-down city shop where he sold trinkets to survive. Since the boy's healing, Jesus had stopped by the shop several times. Christ usually motioned the disciples to pick something out and then told Judas to pay from the bag. The Son of God often lingered after the rest wandered off and chatted easily with the boy about his preteen frustrations and dreams.

Jesus' big smile, long hugs, and encouraging words—"You're very special, you know"—had made a deep impression. The orphan had been struggling to make a miniature boat out of wood, and on one visit Jesus picked it up, looked it over admiringly, then helped him shape a difficult section around the bow. The youngster particularly enjoyed Jesus' stories about His own childhood. One day Christ even brought a package that contained new sandals He had made for the boy.

Now the lad looked through gaps in the angry mob that streamed past his open-air shop and saw the bent and battered frame of his best Friend struggling to keep pace. Instinctively he grabbed an old crutch from under the bench and ran at the soldiers, waving it menacingly over his head. "No! Let Him go! What are you doing! Not Jesus! Please . . . please stop!" he cried, until he was hoarse.

Demetrius

Demetrius, a rather recent recruit to the ranks of the Roman army, was already tired of being dumped on. At age eighteen, his childhood images of heroic soldiers defending the empire had been overshadowed by the barbarous reality of life in the regiment. More screams and brutality had assaulted His naive sensibilities than he had bargained for. Tradition dictated that the lowest in rank got the worst assignments, and lately he had drawn crucifixion detail, at once boring and unnerving.

Demetrius finished breakfast just as an exhausted group of soldiers returned to the barracks after battling the crowds at Jesus' trials. After untying his armor, one veteran commented, "These messiahs are such a stinkin' pain! This one's tough, though, not the usual foul-mouthed whacko. But that crowd's a real zoo for sure!"

The supervisor entered and yelled out, "Demetrius, you've got Calvary again today. Pilate's chosen three for the hill. Two from Barabbas's gang and another self-appointed Deliverer. They've got to be off those crosses by sundown, to keep the finicky Jews happy. Get on with it."

As Demetrius pulled his helmet over his ears, he thought, *Why don't they nail more businessmen. At least I might take home some decent clothing.* He was becoming callused to most aspects of crucifixion, even the pounding of the nails.

He still recoiled, however, at breaking the legs. A crucifixion like this one made it much worse. Usually the victims were so delirious after four or five days on the cross that they didn't react very strongly. Today would be very bad, however. They would be much too alert.

In his imagination Demetrius could already hear the thud of the iron mallet and the appalling crack and crunch and shattering of large bones. He pictured the victim's wild-eyed anticipation, the blood-curdling screams, the writhing and gasping for air, the death spasms. He didn't expect that that would ever become routine.

The soldier who scourged Christ

"Hey, pass that bread over here!" Marcus shouted down the long breakfast table at no one in particular. His large, callused hand clutched a medium-sized loaf of rye that he jammed into his mouth and tore in half with his widely spaced, discolored teeth. White foamy spittle gathered at the corners of his mouth as he chewed hard and bawled out to the other soldiers, "Good day today, boys. Just got word I can cut me up another fanatic Jew. Last week I went too easy on those fools from Jericho. Bad for my reputation. Maybe it was that bruise on my shoulder or somethin'. But I feel good now. Feel the old fire comin' back into these muscles."

Scratching an armpit and smiling broadly, he nodded his head and chortled, "I can hear the snap of the leather already. Yes sir, gonna be a very good day."

He opened and closed his right hand as if squeezing an imaginary ball of leather. The skin on his thick fingers tightened as he periodically held the grip and examined it admiringly from various angles. The only imperfections were the shortened tip of his index finger that had gotten lopped off in a boyhood accident and two deep, jagged scars that crisscrossed near the wrist.

Marcus grabbed an open bottle of cheap barracks wine, shoved the neck deep into his mouth, cocked his head back, and guzzled lustily as his Adam's apple bulged with each new swallow. Finished, he plunked the bottle down loudly and wiped his wet lips with the back of a heavily muscled forearm.

"Why do I get all the good jobs?" he joked. "Must be 'cause I'm so pretty." He choked on his own laughter. With that he pushed away from the aged oak table, grabbed the scourge that lay neatly on his tunic, and lumbered eagerly up the stairs toward Pilate's judgment hall.

The sign maker

Seneca heard loud, insistent banging on the front door of his home. He lay in bed for a few seconds, trying to determine if the noise was real or part of a dream. Again he heard several hard knocks, accompanied by a gruff voice. "Open up, we haven't got much time. Open up in there!"

Seneca rubbed his eyes awake, threw on a robe, and hurried to meet his impatient visitor. "Hello, may I . . . uh . . . may I help you?" he stammered.

A tall, weathered Roman soldier, with a short beard as silver as his armor, pushed his way inside and sat heavily at the table. He moved his sword to one side and then said, "We've got three for Calvary, and I need signs for them all, right away. Listen up now. The first two should each have a couple of words: 'Insurrection' and 'Thief.' That's all. The third is a special order from Pilate, so you'd better get it right. He seemed real particular about this one. He wants it to say, 'Jesus of Nazareth, King of the Jews.' Make all three in the usual languages, Aramaic, Latin, and Greek. You got that straight? Do you?"

Seneca nodded.

"Well, I'll be back shortly," the soldier concluded, and left.

Seneca went to the basin next to his bed, splashed some water on his face, and wiped it off quickly with a towel. He then walked next door to his shop and took three whitewashed boards from the half dozen he kept prepared ahead of time for just such occasions. Each board had two holes with a rope attached so it could be worn around the victim's neck on the way to crucifixion, broadcasting his crime. Seneca laid one board down flat on his workbench and grabbed a chunk of shaped charcoal from a cupboard nearby. Mentally counting the letters in each word, then eyeing the spacing, he hurriedly traced out the guilty verdicts. No time to be fancy. Just good, basic communication.

The first two were relatively easy. The third was more challenging in such limited space. It read:

JESCHUA' NAZORAJA MALKA DIJEHUDAJE
IESUS NAZARENUS REX IUDÆORUM
IGROTR O MAFXQAIOR O BARIKETR SXM IOTDAIXM [2]

Seneca brought the signs back to his home and stood them up against the wall next to the door. He rested and reflected on how this little extra money was coming at just the right time. He liked it when Roman orders came in batches like this, instead of just one victim at a time. Hardly worth the trouble otherwise. After downing some bread and wine, he stared over at the finished boards and commented to his wife, "This King's apparently gonna have two of his vice presidents in crime with him on the hill today. Maybe they're gonna hold a special cabinet meeting up there or something," he chuckled.

The women

Many women were drawn to Jesus' message because of the value that He placed on them as persons. He cared for their needs with dignity and grace. Though not yet full followers, four of these women were neighbors and close personal friends. Earlier that week they had witnessed His triumphal entry. Yet, knowing the hatred and power of the Jewish leaders, they could not shake a vague sense of dread. Ominous rumors were rampant.

On the Friday of the crucifixion, the four women separately heard the news of Christ's arrest and conviction. Within minutes they gathered in one of the homes, anxious and disbelieving. One woman said, "My husband, Rubin, heard talk of crucifixion! *How could they? Jesus is such a kind man!*"

Another offered, "Perhaps it isn't true at all. Maybe it's just more Jewish propaganda. You know how things get blown out of proportion around here."

They threw on shawls and headed toward the city, about a mile away. The cloudless sky and pleasant singing of the birds calmed their fears somewhat. Then they saw it . . . the procession. Roman spears encircled a trio of condemned men, one of which was clearly Christ. The women raced toward the surreal scene. The mob, at least fifteen people deep on each side, snaked far back down the slope. As the women pressed in, their senses were bombarded by the swirl of loud taunts and curses mingled with the unmistakable stench of life from the streets.

Caught up in a moving tangle of elbows and feet, one woman was shoved rudely to the ground, and she screamed. Another, barely able to keep her balance, was hemmed in and swept along with the flow of humanity. The two others eventually struggled through to the inner corridor just as Jesus drew near. They shouted His name while tears coursed down their cheeks. An involuntary wail burst from their lips. Christ glanced over, squinting through blood and sweat, and declared, " 'Daughters of Jerusalem, do not weep for Me, but weep for yourselves and for your children' "[3] (Luke 23:28). The women reached out with futile gestures then turned aside, weeping hysterically.

The carpenter/blacksmith

The city carpenter who supplied wooden crosses to the Romans inwardly detested his alliance with the foreigners, but the money was good and the work steady. With six kids, he had to put food on the table. Jesus had once stopped by his shop to talk casually about wood and the winds of change. Over the last two years, when crowds gathered outside town to hear Jesus speak, this man had often lingered at the fringes. He was intrigued by the uncommon spiritual wisdom of a fellow craftsman. He could sense his own view of God changing. It made him more gentle and caring. His relationship with his wife and kids definitely improved as a result.

Jesus' death procession now passed quite near this man's shop, and the carpenter peered out upon the chaotic events. He then saw that it was Christ who would be hung on one of the crossbars he himself had fashioned! His stomach tightened as he moved closer to the window and squinted into the bright morning sun. A Roman soldier suddenly entered the shop and demanded more spikes. The man hesitated but relented at the raising of a spear. He tossed a handful of large nails into a bucket and reluctantly handed them over. Stung by regret, he stepped outside just in time to see the soldier hurry through the city gate on the way to Golgotha.

Deborah

Thirty-eight-year-old Deborah belonged to the Society of Mercy, a group of volunteer Jewish women dedicated to easing the pain inflicted by Rome. The group of twenty-three women was powerless to throw off the Roman yoke but did what little they could to soften the empire's evil. Among other things, this first-century Red Cross carefully monitored the activity on Golgotha and offered victims a homemade drug of wine liberally mixed with myrrh. Prisoners eagerly sought the bitter-tasting brew to mitigate the fiery bolts of pain from nerves sliced through by nails. Before the spikes were hammered in, the soldiers usually allowed the society a few minutes to come near.

Word passed to Deborah about 8:00 A.M. that three men would be crucified in an hour. She put aside her Passover preparations and hastened to the back of a friend's shop, where the society kept most of its supplies. Grabbing a bottle of wine, a cup, and key ingredients, she made her way through the crowded city streets and up the winding, rocky pathway toward Calvary. She arrived shortly before Jesus' procession and was grateful for a few moments to gather her thoughts and steel herself for the all-too-familiar events to come.

"The sky is too blue, and the clouds are too elegant to be a canopy for such an awful place," she mused. Her eyes scanned the half-dozen holes drilled in the stone summit for multiple crosses. The area around each hole was stained by a random pattern of reddish-brown dried blood. The slight breeze carried the unmistakable leftover stench of death.

Deborah mixed the pain-lessening potion then peered nervously toward the well-worn route that led up from the city. Approaching shouts and the rhythmic tramp of soldiers' feet caused her fingers to tighten around the wine bottle. Jesus crested the hill first, with Simon of Cyrene immediately behind, laboring under the imposed cross. Soldiers surrounded them. Next the two thieves arrived—staggering under their own load, red faced, breathing heavily, with sweat dripping off their chins.

The soldiers removed the crossbeams then motioned Deborah forward. She offered the anesthetic to Christ, who looked up with swollen, bloodshot eyes, whispered a hoarse Thank you, but shook His head No. She paused, with a quizzical look, still holding the cup out in front of her. No one had ever refused before. After a few moments she turned and approached the thieves. The taller one snatched the cup from her hands and drank eagerly, begging for more. The other thief elbowed him aside, scolding, "That's enough!"[4] (See Mark 15:23; Matthew 27:34.)

Caleb and Naomi

A turnpike into Jerusalem ran only a stone's throw from Calvary. On Friday the thoroughfare bore thousands pouring into the city for Passover. Caleb, his wife, Naomi, and their two small sons, ages 6 and 9, were traveling the road on the final leg of their first pilgrimage. Months of planning and three weeks of wearisome walking had brought them within sight of Jerusalem's high city walls and magnificent temple dome. They stopped on the crest of a hill to rest and revel in their accomplishment.

"I'm so happy for the boys. What a wonderful learning opportunity!" Naomi exclaimed. After downing figs, bread, and water, they again joined the throng streaming along the crowded road. The eldest son spotted Golgotha first. It was nearly 10:00 A.M., and the victims had been on display for about an hour.

Pointing, the boy inquired, "What's happening on that hill, Dad? Are those real nails holding them up there?"

When Naomi saw the crucifixion, her mind raced back to her own childhood. Roman soldiers had wreaked revenge on her rural village because of rumors that some inhabitants were stealing food from an army warehouse nearby. Local Roman sympathizers delighted in fabricating guilt. Five innocent men were hastily and savagely crucified in the town square.

"Caleb, take the boys away. Hurry!" Naomi cried. She turned them back toward the city and pushed each one on ahead.

"Daddy, what did those men do?" the youngest boy pressed.

Yanking both boys by the arm, Caleb stole another glance. He could hear one of the victims cursing loudly. *Poor wretches,* he thought. *Romans! Of all days. Too bad the kids had to see that.*

The thief's mother

Not every onlooker at Calvary had come there because of Jesus. A widow, Ruth, drew near to grieve for her youngest son, Samuel, who hung on his own miserable cross. Months earlier twenty-three-year-old Samuel had expressed interest in Jesus' message. On several occasions he sought out Christ and listened carefully to His hope-filled words.

Ruth delighted in the obvious effect on Samuel's life. Normally sullen and withdrawn, he now seemed so much more optimistic and self-confident. One day, however, Samuel innocently quizzed a Jewish scribe about one of Jesus' parables. The next day several Pharisee leaders visited the young man, admonished him to reject this "false Messiah," and warned of dire consequences if he refused.

Samuel felt trapped between two vital yet conflicting loyalties. Anger and depression enveloped him. To stifle the pleadings of the Spirit, he decided to abandon not only Christ but also religion altogether.[5] He began hanging around a neighborhood gang that robbed for sport. He eventually fell in with Barabbas, a natural leader and self-proclaimed deliverer of Israel. One day, Samuel found himself in the chaos of a downtown riot against Rome, during which Barabbas went berserk and murdered a soldier. Samuel and another cohort were swept up in the authorities' net, then convicted and sentenced to the nails.

As the soldiers on Golgotha wrestled Samuel to the ground, he glanced over at his mother with a look of wild-eyed desperation. Ruth let out an involuntary gasp. Shortly after the cross was raised, all her son's pent-up anger and confusion suddenly burst forth. Ruth was shocked to hear the stream of obscenities that poured from Samuel's lips as he railed against Christ and Judaism.

Her heart broke as she looked up into the bitter, anxious face of her vilified son. Things could have been so very different. Self-recrimination tortured her spirit. What else could she have done? She felt the searing, accusing eyes of relatives and acquaintances who had stopped by to shake their heads and stare. Later, after a long period of silence, her son spoke once again, this time in subdued but earnest tones, as a suppliant. Ruth strained to hear his final words: " 'Lord, remember me when You come in Your Kingdom.' "

Mary

However Jesus' mother heard the news of His arrest, it probably did not come to her as a complete surprise. Things had been going downhill for months. The Jewish leaders' bitter reaction to the triumphal entry filled Mary's heart with dread. Jesus' casting out the money-changers only poured fuel on the flames.

Why does He have to stir them up so? she thought. *If only Joseph were here, perhaps he could talk some sense into Him.*

All week Christ had confronted the Pharisees openly. The last verbal battle was, without question, the worst. With hundreds of people crowding the temple courts, Jesus glared at the venerated Jewish leaders and shouted, " 'Woe unto you, scribes and Pharisees, hypocrites! Woe unto you, blind guides!' " Why did He have to say things in such a pointed way?

Learning of Jesus' arrest shortly after 1:00 A.M., Mary buried her head in her hands, slumped onto her narrow bed, and wept. Later a neighbor dropped by. Mary sat quietly, staring into the night, as if looking far away. Suddenly she said, "I must go and see for myself. Please come with me."

Donning woolen cloaks and scarves, they stepped out into the dangerous night. Along the road, Mary's mind tried to anticipate what lay ahead. She shivered with more than the early morning chill. Just outside the heavy city gates there was relative quiet. After entering, Mary somehow met the apostle John and queried him for every possible shred of information.

He attempted to comfort her, but she sensed the anxiety that lay beneath his carefully chosen words. John hurried back to Jesus' trial, promising to return. The night eventually built to a crescendo of terrible news. By 8:00 A.M. Mary needed no messenger. She circled the crowd that screamed for Barabbas and listened in horror as Pilate condemned her precious boy to the cross. Staring back into the apostle's tear-filled eyes, she cried out, "Crucifixion! Oh no, John! Not crucifixion!"

Later, John placed his arm over Mary's shoulder as they followed Jesus' mournful procession toward Calvary. As the two thieves were fixed to the trees, she looked on in agonized suspense. Would Jesus actually allow Himself to be crucified? Were all her hopes and dreams to be executed as well? She had outlived her husband; would she now outlive her beloved Son? Nausea crept through her system as her mind attempted to grasp the awful reality. She reached out to John for support as her knees weakened and a cold sweat bathed her form.

"She saw His hands stretched upon the cross; the hammer and the nails were brought, and as the spikes were driven through the tender flesh, the heart-stricken disciples bore away from the cruel scene the fainting form of the mother of Jesus."[6]

At a nearby home, friends tried to comfort Mary. "He's in God's hands now. Jesus can still manifest His power. It may not be too late." She remained inconsolable.

Later, the apostle John, realizing the end was getting near, found Mary and urged her to return to Golgotha.[7] Emerging unsteadily atop the hill, Mary drew as near as possible to the middle cross. How Christ had withered in such a short time! Her son's life was clearly ebbing away. Jesus looked down at her, then over at John and said with considerable difficulty, " 'Behold your mother; woman, behold your son.' " Mary let out an audible gasp and turned away.

Miriam

Miriam, her husband, and their only son, Korath, had joined hundreds of others seeking a miracle. A stream of human suffering hobbled and dragged itself toward Jerusalem, where Jesus was reported to be staying. Korath burned with fever and was frequently convulsed by interminable seizures. This twelve-year-old now weighed a frightening fifty pounds and did not have long to live. The family had traveled for days, wending their way toward the distant city, inspired by the testimony of relatives from the south. Jesus was their only chance.

Each day of the journey brought them in contact with still more people who had recently experienced Christ's gentle healing hand. Miriam's heart strengthened with hope. She dared to smile again in anticipation of renewed vigor. Maybe Korath would grow up to be an artisan! Perhaps she would rejoice at his wedding and cuddle his children after all.

The final day of their journey brought them to the gates of the city just before Sabbath. They inquired eagerly of Jesus' whereabouts. Then the terrible, heartbreaking news: "He was crucified earlier today. He died only two hours ago. They've already wrapped His body and taken Him to the tomb. He's gone."

Miriam would not allow herself to believe the dreadful report. She cupped her hands over her ears and shook her head while the people recounted the deeds of the day. Her voice choked with tears as she insisted on seeing Jesus.

"With persistent earnestness they asked for Him. They would not be turned away. Soldiers were stationed . . . to keep back the multitude that came with their sick and dying, demanding entrance."[8]

Eventually, however, reality suffocated Miriam's hope. "The sufferers who had come to be healed by the Savior sank under their disappointment. The streets were filled with mourning. The sick were dying for want of the healing touch of Jesus."[9]

You

You race into the city of Jerusalem and work your way cautiously over to the edge of the large mob that has gathered in front of the Roman Praetorium. The rabble is in a very ugly mood. "What's happening?" you inquire of no one in particular.

A bulky, unkempt man with a raspy voice and tangled, greasy hair turns and snickers as he replies, "They're about to bring that lunatic messiah out here again. That guy really needs to be taught a lesson, a big lesson." He spits on the ground and continues, "I really hate impostors like him." After a brief glance back at the judgment hall, he looks you over more closely and asks, "What do you think about this Nazarene clown anyway?" You think carefully before replying.

1. Ellen G. White, *Redemption or The Sufferings of Christ, His Trial and Crucifixion*, 72.
2. Josef Blinzler, *The Trial of Jesus*, 254.
3. *The Desire of Ages*, 742, 743.
4. Barclay, *The Gospel of Mark*, 361.
5. *The Desire of Ages,* 749.
6. Ibid., 744.
7. Ibid., 752.
8. Ibid., 776.
9. Ibid.

Chapter 6

The Pain of Verbal Abuse

For years there was one aspect of Jesus' sufferings that I read over much too quickly. I failed to give adequate weight to the horrible verbal abuse heaped upon Him from Gethsemane to the cross. I knew about the mockery and slander in general terms. But not until I examined the various incidents in detail did I begin to see this as a very significant source of pain. Over and over again during that terrible nightmare, Jesus was subjected to verbal onslaughts that would have withered the strongest of men. Mouths spat obscenities forged in evil.

I used to think that Jesus had a sort of heavenly thick skin when it came to taunts and verbal abuse. But His great love actually made Him unusually sensitive to ill treatment. Note the following from the Spirit of Prophecy:

> *Christ suffered keenly under abuse and insult.* At the hands of the beings whom He had created, and for whom He was making an infinite sacrifice, He received every indignity. And He suffered in proportion to the perfection of His holiness and His hatred of sin. His trial by men who acted as fiends was to Him a perpetual sacrifice. To be surrounded by human beings under the control of Satan was revolting to Him.[1]

He suffered to the same degree that He loved. He ached with the same intensity that He hated sin. Jesus' spirit was wounded and torn by the venom that spewed forth from His creation. Based on the Bible and the Spirit of Prophecy, we will try to imagine what such awful abuse might have been like by reconstructing certain scenes and dialogue.

I have divided the verbal abuse into four different categories:

1. Angry accusations
2. Interrogation and threats
3. Rejection and condemnation
4. Mockery

I have given only a few samples of the many incidents that could have been selected under each category. The types of verbal abuse covered here were repeated over and over in various forms from Gethsemane to the cross. The purpose of this chapter is to draw the reader more fully into the scenes in order to increase our appreciation of what Christ endured.

1. Angry accusations

At the first Sanhedrin trial

Torches cast an eerie light around the large, ornate room within the Jewish judgment hall as certain Sanhedrists gathered for the initial trial of Jesus. Both Annas and Caiaphas had privately tried to elicit incriminating information from Christ, but in vain.[2] Now, with acute feelings of disgust and frustration, Caiaphas gathered his priestly robes about him and ceremoniously took his seat as presiding officer.

Jewish elders, judges, other assorted hypocrites, and irritated soldiers watched with intense interest as the renegade Rabbi was roughly ushered into their midst. Encircled by sharp spears and angry spectators, the Son of God took in the scene, heaved a deep, grief-stricken sigh, and hung His head in silent resignation.

After a few explanatory remarks, Caiaphas instructed, "Bring in the first witness."

A tall, lean, scruffy-looking man with a suspiciously new robe took his position near the judges. "What's your accusation, sir?" Caiaphas intoned expectantly.

"I don't want no trouble," he began. "I'm a peaceable man, but I figure I gotta speak out. Somebody's gotta tell the truth. I hear lots of things on the street, you know, lots of things. And I hear that this terrorist is tryin' to start a full-scale rebellion, an uprisin'. He's been stirrin' people up for months. Why, His followers had swords in the garden this very night!

"He's been secretly settin' the stage for trouble, gatherin' more and more supporters. And He's always talkin' about settin' up His own kingdom. Just this last weekend He rode into the city on a donkey, like a king, like royalty or somethin'. Thousands were yellin' and screamin', 'Hosanna' and callin' Him the King of Israel. This thing is about to explode, I tell ya!

"I know for certain that He wants to overthrow Pilate and set up a rival government. I'm sure of it. But he'll get us nothin' but Roman vengeance! He's poison, I tell ya, poison! I wrote Him off as a dreamer at first, but now this whole thing's gettin' outta control. I got a family to worry about, your honor. We got enough trouble around here without this idiot. For the sake of our nation, this assembly has a sacred duty, a duty to God, to rid us of dangerous fanatics like this Jesus."

Voices murmured assent as Caiaphas thanked the witness for his courage in speaking out. Turning his gaze directly at Jesus, the high priest leaned forward and spat out his inquiry, "What about it, Rabbi? We've had enough of your lies. Your real ambitions are out in the open now. What do you have to say? Speak!"

The next witness, an elderly man with piercing eyes and a large mane of distinguished-looking gray hair, was motioned out from the waiting area behind long red drapes. Hobbling forward, he gazed around the room as if awed by the splendid surroundings. Caiaphas then solicited his accusations with unusual politeness.

The man stroked his beard nervously as he spoke. "I've been a shop owner in this city for many years, your holiness, and nothing much of any importance goes on without me catching wind of it. I've seen self-styled deliverers come and go, you know, lots of them. Thankfully, most of them are now rotting in the ground or rotting in Roman jails. Good riddance, I say, let 'em rot. But this joker right here is the worst, by far. No question. He's not just a big-mouthed braggart. He's a madman."

The witness stepped to the side slightly and turned to face Jesus, pointing at Him periodically as he continued. "I have direct evidence that this man is planning on destroying our magnificent temple here in Jerusalem. It makes no sense, but I heard Him with my own ears. Heard it plain as day. Said he'd tear the whole temple down, right to the ground, one stone after the other. Don't ask me how or why, but I believe He's crazy enough to try it. And he's got hundreds of low-life followers that would be more than happy to join in.

"He has no regard for our temple, none at all. Just look at how He desecrated the temple a few days ago, throwing out all those legitimate businesses that have been there for years. I have friends whose goods He scattered and ruined. They're fine, honest people who were treated like thieves.

"There's nothin' more sacred to my heart, your honor, than that temple over there. Thousands come from hundreds of miles away just to see it, just like they're doing today for Passover." Pursing his lips and glaring in disgust, the witness shook his fist vigorously and yelled, "No one, no one, should talk about damaging that temple in any way and live. This sacred council has got to stop this renegade right here and now!

"And to show you how crazy this fool really is, He said that after destroying the temple He'd put it all back together, better 'n new, in just three little days. Herod's been building that temple for over forty years, and he's talking seventy-two hours" (See John 2:20, KJV.) "He's a nut case, your honor. I'm telling you, the man is evil. If you care anything about our nation, our security, you gotta get rid of him before it's too late." He paused for effect, bowed deeply to Caiaphas and the judges, then left.

One by one the witnesses came, making the most of their moment in the lime-light. Full of self-importance, they implicated Christ in the most heinous schemes. Caiaphas soon realized, however, that his witnesses were eager but uncoordinated. No two pieces fit together. The impression was one of hasty fabrication.

Furious, the high priest waved back the next witness and turned to Jesus Himself with renewed determination. "This august assembly cannot allow your seditious influence to go unchecked. You have obviously stirred up dangerous controversy and discontent. You're a no-good rebel! There are even reports that you've been corrupting our children with your fanatical teachings. It's our duty to get the truth. Do you want your family excommunicated? Do you want your degenerate disciples rounded up and locked away? All these troublemakers must be rooted out. Admit your role, and we'll forget the others."

The high priest's face flushed deep red with anger at Christ's persistent silence. Beside himself with indignation, Caiaphas pounded the arm of his chair, stood up, and screamed out, "Speak, you coward! Do you answer nothing to all these charges? By the God of heaven, speak!" The words of rage echoed throughout the hallowed hall. A stunned hush fell over the gathering. Sweating profusely, the venerated leader sucked in great gulps of air, gathering strength for a still more impassioned and desperate attack.[3] (See Matthew 26:57-66; Mark 14:53-64.)

2. Interrogation and threats
The trial before Herod
The hazy morning sun began to coax dew off the pavement and warm the leftover chill as Jesus was shoved and jostled the few hundred yards to Herod's

sumptuous palace. Noisy shouts and cries jarred upon the early morning quiet. Great ornate doors were opened, and from an anteroom to the left Herod entered his famous courtroom where too many infamous decisions had already been made.

"Well, here you are," Herod began. "Jesus. Jesus of Nazareth." Leaning back in his splendid throne, the prophet killer crossed his legs casually and sized up the Son of God. "You're not as tall as I expected. Not as regal either. Nasty wounds you've got there. You must have made somebody mighty upset. Really now, I'd like to get acquainted. Tell me something about yourself. Upbringing, goals. How did a carpenter decide to become a rabbi?"

There followed a long string of varied questions, each of which was answered by Christ with painful silence. "You may not have gone to Jewish schools, but surely you learned how to talk," the king continued with growing irritation. "Has that tongue of yours stopped working? Don't be nervous. Tell me now what you believe, what you teach; I'm interested. What's your goal—power, prestige, money—what? Why are you making all these waves around here and upsetting the authorities?" Herod's words faded until the only sound was that of his fingers drumming on the armrest in angry agitation.

"OK. Actions speak louder than words anyway. Bring in that bunch of cripples," he ordered, pointing to a nearby alcove. A hastily gathered group of maimed victims from the alley hobbled forward. "Now, mister powerful, mister miracle worker, give us a demonstration to prove your claims. Heal these poor wretches."

The thought that Christ might impress Herod and gain His release sent the Jewish priests and rulers into frenzied action. "Your highness," they quickly shouted, "we know this man. We've questioned him thoroughly. His claims are the groundless boasts of a hothead. This coward should not be permitted to pollute your great courtroom. He is a disgrace to Judaism, O king, and a traitor. Lies and secrecy are His tools. It is well He doesn't speak, for His mouth is capable of nothing but blasphemy! Whatever miracles he performs are through the power of the evil one. He is foul, poison. Spells can be cast and demon influences set loose!" As if on cue, well-orchestrated bedlam erupted almost instantly.

Herod leapt to his feet, shouting, "Enough, enough! Quiet! Every one of you, quiet!" Soldiers quickly restored order. Turning to Jesus once again, Herod threatened Him with condemnation unless He answered. "I am the one with the authority in this courtroom. You are nothing. Your life is in my hands. You are a mere ant to be squashed underfoot if I choose. Where did you get all your rebel ideas? Who do you think you are, taking on the whole Jewish establishment, and now Rome? Do you have any brains, or is your head full of rocks?"

Christ, His eyes now fixed on Herod's face, didn't respond. The king shouted, "You fool! I'll make you talk. No one, no one refuses my will. Answer me . . . now!" Christ turned His gaze far off into the distance, as if oblivious to the king's tirade.

Beside himself with rage, Herod threatened Christ again with torture and even death. "You scum. How dare you defy me! Your head will come off just as easily as John's." Standing directly in front of Jesus, the king shouted, "You fake. You no-good imposter! The crowd will teach you how to behave before royalty. Let's see if you can work a miracle now to save your miserable messianic neck!"[4] (See Luke 23:6-12.)

3. Rejection and condemnation

Jesus was the bravest of all Sufferers, but He who loved life and lived it so abundantly must have been inwardly convulsed when condemned to die. How such a verdict must have slammed against His sensitive soul! It would be unrealistic to say the Author of life was unmoved by the anticipation of death. To Him death was utterly foreign and repulsive; it violated all that was within Him.

On humanity's most disgraceful night, Jesus heard calls for His death up to ten separate times. The cumulative effect of such repeated rejection and judgment by His own beloved creation must have tormented His emotions unmercifully.

Most Americans remember well the prolonged Iranian hostage crisis during the Carter presidency. Video footage pictured the blindfolded hostages being shoved through cluttered streets where thousands of furious Iranian citizens chanted, "Death to the Americans! Death to the Americans!" After their release, many of the hostages reported that the incessant threats of mob violence and death were the most difficult part of their experience. For them to be at the mercy of such erratic, bloodthirsty forces, so far from home and safety, was mentally and emotionally devastating.

So it must have been for Christ! Even though He had the power to lay His tormentors in the dust, He also knew He could not use that power in His own behalf. It is certainly far more difficult to submit to abuse and condemnation when you can free yourself so easily!

Imagine a father who has raised his children magnificently. The kids have been the love of his life. One day, after his children are grown, this father is falsely accused in a terrible scandal that has the local community up in arms. As he ascends the courthouse steps with his lawyer, the dad hears an angry, though familiar, voice above the hostile crowd that presses in around him. He looks back and sees his own beautiful daughter jabbing a finger at him angrily, yelling, "You murderer! You're nothing but dirt! The electric chair would be too merciful for you!" The terrible, unfair scandal itself has torn his heart, but now this. It is too much. For Jesus, every face in the crowd was like that son or daughter!

The second trial before Pilate

By the time the guards returned with Christ from Herod's Palace, the crowd at Pilate's judgment hall had swelled dramatically. The people were climbing on colonnades, standing on benches, sitting on shoulders, straining for a better view. The smell of blood hovered in the air, and a lynch-mob mentality gripped the multitude. It was the adrenaline-pumping prospect of witnessing someone else's pain. Roman justice could create quite a spectacle.

Near the middle of the crowd, Rabbi Ben Hannan and his friends from the Sanhedrin peered over people's heads and saw, far down in front, the purple-robed, hunched figure of Pilate striding into view, gesturing in annoyance at the mob to be quiet. On either side of the governor stood at least thirty armor-clad soldiers outfitted with swords or grasping long silver-tipped spears. About three hundred thickly muscled troops patrolled the edges of the vast open plaza.

Rabbi Ben Hannan squinted into the early morning sun, trying to shield his eyes with his right hand. After hearing Pilate declare earlier, " 'I find no fault in this man,' " he had become alarmed at the possibility of Jesus' release. Now, while Pilate hesitated to act, Ben Hannan and his fellow priests set aside their normal religious reserve and hurriedly fanned out to work the sprawling crowd.[5]

"How can Rome let this fanatic go free?" they asked the people nearby. "Caesar will crush us all if he catches wind of Jesus' deeds. Better for this imposter to die than for the whole nation to be slaughtered. Are you going to let this fake Messiah get away with this? Are you?" Their incendiary sentiments inflamed the people's passions into a swirling frenzy. Hateful words raced throughout the vast assembly.

Soon the Roman governor's hoarse voice rang out over the Praetorium, " 'Whom will ye that I release unto you? Barabbas, or Jesus which is called Christ?' " (Matthew 27:17, KJV). Ben Hannan once again sprang into immediate action. Cupping his hands over his bearded mouth, he yelled at the top of his lungs, "Release Barabbas! Barabbas!" Other Sanhedrists chimed in as if on cue. The spark caught fire and grew into a roaring chant from hundreds of voices, "Barabbas, Barabbas!"

At Pilate's inquiry, " 'What shall I do then with Jesus which is called Christ?' " the multitudes screamed back the dreadful reply, " 'Let him be crucified!' " (verse 22, KJV).

Still trying desperately to release Christ, Pilate said, "I will chastise him and let him go."

At the words "let him go," the huge mob erupted. "Crucify Him . . . Crucify! . . . Crucify! . . . Crucify!" they screamed over and over, louder and still louder. Little children put their hands over their ears at the deafening chant. Women drew their shawls tightly over their heads. Pilate himself took a couple of steps backward as if hit by a hot, evil wind. Soldiers tightened their ranks and raised their spears higher, sensing that the seething cauldron of hate could boil over at any moment. Christ gazed out at the women and children in the crowd, and tears welled up in His swollen, bloodshot eyes.

There was a sudden hush as Jesus was tied to a pillar on stage, and scourged. At each stroke of the lash the crowd cheered with raucous delight. "Harder . . . rip Him . . . punish the troublemaker!"

Several soldiers then led the Son of God away inside the hall. The Savior reappeared about thirty to forty minutes later, sporting more injuries and a ridiculous-looking crown of long, razor-sharp thorns. Someone pulled His robe down, exposing the flayed flesh of the upper body. Pilate displayed Christ as one might a pathetic sideshow freak.

Jesus was shoved toward the crowd, and He stumbled forward. Blood streamed down His face, neck, shoulders, back, and legs, matting His hair and beard, decorating His torso in shiny crimson ribbons. The Son of God tilted His head down to allow the blood to spill off His forehead rather than running into His eyes. Murderous Barabbas was brought alongside and easily won the popularity contest for release.

Another plea for mercy from Pilate only threw gas on the fires of animosity, infuriating the mob even further, ratcheting up their anger to new, intoxicating heights. The raw, maddened cry, "Crucify Him, Crucify the imposter," again exploded upon the fine, sunlit day. The very ground seemed to vibrate with the noise.[6] (see Matthew 27:20-23; Mark 15:6-14; Luke 23:13-23; John 18:38-19:15).

4. Mockery

I feel that I can speak with some insight concerning the sting of mockery, having been the primary target of a bully's ridicule during four very difficult teenage years. From the sixth grade through the ninth, he regularly managed to find something about my looks, clothing, words, activities, and ancestry to publicly put down. I give him high marks for creativity and intimidation. He seemed to tower over me like a giant who took boxing lessons. (No kid in the neighborhood dared oppose him except the amazing Johnny Parker). I have no idea why this pubescent menace focused so intently on me, but I can still remember all too easily my feelings of raw hate and fear. Oh, how it all hurt!

All that time, no one in my family knew of my torment until the day I snapped and recklessly "ordered" the bully to meet me at the playground that coming Friday at 3:00 P.M. to settle the matter once and for all. In preparation, I held mock fights in front of my bedroom mirror, trying in vain to teach myself how to throw a decent punch. I could only dream of beating him, and I knew it.

That Friday I showed up at the playground alone like a lamb to the slaughter, overcome with dread. Rambo came over the horizon with two scowling assistants. The battle was soon joined, and I got creamed. My father found me at suppertime sprawled on my bed with facial bruises, sore muscles, a broken tooth, and an ego in the minus fifty range. One phone call from Dad, however, quickly put an end to my very long ordeal.

With an inner pain infinitely greater than I ever experienced, and with a yearning love for His enemies I did not possess, Christ suffered immensely under insult and ridicule. The tongue can be a far more potent weapon than whip or club. Ellen White observes,

> [Christ] was not insensible to ignominy [shame] and contempt; he submitted to it, *but he felt its bitterness as no other being could feel it.* Pure, holy, and undefiled, he was yet arraigned as criminal before the eyes of the world. From the highest exaltation the adorable Redeemer took step after step in the path of humiliation.[7]

Mockery strives to strip its victim of all semblance of dignity and worth. Jesus felt the torment of derision all His life. Evil men heaped on Christ "all the contempt of which human beings, inspired by Satan, are capable."[8] The final episodes of ridicule began the moment He was arrested in Gethsemane and continued until He died. During the last hours of His life, the Son of God was subjected to intense, painful mockery numerous times. The following three scenes give us glimpses into what He endured.

Roman soldiers in the Praetorium

At one point in the Roman trial, Pilate's guards took Jesus to the barracks yard for a period of raucous mockery and ridicule. Such horseplay provided comic relief from the grind and discipline of military life. As many as two hundred soldiers gathered, forming a circle fourteen or fifteen deep around the Savior. Most viewed Christ as simply another local idiot whose big mouth had gotten Him in hot water with the authorities.

"Quiet! Shut up, you guys!" an officer yelled to the troops. "We have a rare opportunity here to welcome a visiting dignitary to our party, a king no less, king of these pain-in-the-neck Jews. You know that Messiah they've been waiting for, the fellow who's supposed to exterminate us? This is the one! This is their conqueror, so be very cautious around him. On such short notice he forgot his fancy kingly robe, so we've taken the liberty of employing this slightly used one here. He's holy, they tell us, so what could be more fitting than all these rips and holes?"

"Hail, O king of holes," someone yelled. Laughter rippled throughout the ranks.

A stool was commandeered, and someone shoved the Savior onto it as a makeshift throne. A handsome young soldier pushed his way through the other men and yelled, "Look, I've made the perfect crown." Standing next to Christ, he held the thorny ring up high for all to see then ceremoniously pressed it onto Jesus' head. He wiggled it around somewhat as if to get a better fit and then stood back to admire his work. "May this crown be the beginning of a very happy and extremely fruitful reign," he sneered.

"Only one thing's missing," another continued. "Someone give me that stick over there." A four-foot long reed was hurled over heads and snatched by a soldier. He bent over, opened Jesus' right hand, then wrapped the Savior's fingers around the pretend scepter as one might do in helping a little child.

"Awesome, isn't he? Look out, Caesar! Tremble, mighty Rome!" he exclaimed.

Several came forward, thumped their right arm diagonally across their chest in salute, bowed their head, then knelt down on one knee and hollered, "Hail, King of the Jews." Before rising they paused to spit in Jesus' face, each time causing the delighted throng to burst out in cheers.

Others picked up on Christ's claim to be the Son of God and bowed in turn before Him with offerings of trash from a nearby rubbish barrel—"O great god of rotten wood. O lord of morons and fools. Accept these, our humble gifts."

"Oh no . . . the royal robe! You're messing up his royal garments," someone observed wryly. "His queen mother won't like this one single bit."

"No problem," another replied, "I hear she gave birth to this dummy right in the middle of filth. He's used to it."[9] (See Matthew 27:27-31; Mark 15:16-19; John 19:2, 3.)

The mob around Christ as He struggled to carry His cross

Time became a blur to Jesus as part of the cross was laid on His raw and bleeding shoulders. After a few wobbly steps He crumpled heavily to the ground. This became an unexpected source of amusement for the onlookers, and they almost doubled over in laughter at His awful plight.

"Hey, mister carpenter, haven't you ever carried a real piece of lumber before?"

"Didn't Joseph teach you to handle a piece of wood better than that?" another shouts.

"Do you plan on crawling all the way up to Golgotha, Mister Messiah? That'll take forever. We haven't got all day. Look at those other two thieves carrying their crosses so beautifully, what's the matter with you? Get up and put some life in those steps. Make your mommy proud of you for once in your life."

Christ was whipped to His feet and staggered a few more yards, weaving unsteadily from one side to the other. "Look out, stand back, this joker can't even walk a straight line. Must have been into the wine again. Make way for the King of drunks."

Once again the heavy beam proved too much for the Savior in His weakened condition. He collapsed to the ground, and the mockery of the crowd was stirred anew. "I thought you taught that your burden was light?" someone yelled. "What strength! What stamina! That's it, fall down on those knees, mister holy man, and pray! See if heaven cares about scum like you!"[10]

Jesus' enemies on Calvary

As Jesus hung on the cross, bleeding and gasping for air, the mob and the Jewish leaders had a field day mocking and ridiculing Him.

One of the many onlookers pointed at Christ and yelled, "What happened to all your boasting, Mr. Carpenter? How can you destroy our great temple and build it again from up there? Can I get you a hammer so you can take out those nasty nails?" Hearty laughter rippled through the crowd.

Someone else cupped their hands over their mouth and shouted, "For a wretch like you to claim to be Israel's holy Messiah makes me sick. Son of God? You're the son of passion, the son of Mary's lust!"

A Pharisee, who had been present earlier in the week when Jesus denounced his kind as hypocrites and vipers, eagerly approached the cross. "Who is being denounced now, Mr. Holy Man? Who is the evil one this day?" He paused briefly, then hurled sarcasm at the Savior. "King Jesus, that's not a very nice throne you have there. Can't you find something a little more regal looking and respectable? Something a little more comfortable? Where is your kingdom, anyway, in that dump over there?"

A tall scribe with a thick beard joined in the fun, "If you come down from that cross, I'll be the first to believe in you. I promise. Come down here, and I'll bow on these wobbly knees right there, on that bloody rock. I challenge you to prove to us right now that you aren't a fake. Prove you aren't some pitiful joke. Make your followers proud of you today, Jesus, by getting off that shameful piece of wood."

One of the long-time members of the Sanhedrin added, "You call God your Father? Well, where is He? If you trust Him and know Him so well, why doesn't He deliver you? You claim to be His Son, but surely He wouldn't let His Son be treated like this? He hasn't forgotten you, has He? The truth is that you are a disgrace to God and to our religion. You are a blasphemer and a fool."[11] (See Matthew 27:39-44; Mark 15:29-32; Luke 23:35-38.)

---

1. *The Desire of Ages*, 700, italics supplied.
2. Ibid., 699, 703.
3. Ibid., 704-709
4. Ibid., 728-731.
5. Ibid., 733.
6. Ibid., 731-737.
7. Ellen G. White, "The Plan of Salvation," *Signs of the Times,* 20 Feb. 1893, italics supplied.
8. *Seventh-day Adventist Bible Commentary*, 7A:687.
9. *The Desire of Ages*, 734.
10. Ibid., 742.
11. Ibid., 746-750.

Chapter 7

The Pain of Our Own Self-Destruction

One of Christ's most difficult problems all during His lifetime was the fact that He was capable of feeling too much sorrow. Christ had the heart of God housed in the body of a man. Therefore His sorrow always had the lethal potential of intensifying far beyond the capacity of His mind and body to endure it, which in fact happened in Gethsemane and on the cross.

Our family once lived in a tired old house where the electrical circuit had the aggravating habit of periodically delivering way too much current to the light bulbs. At times the energy was so intense that it actually resulted in the bulbs' early demise. The mysterious overload was no respecter of bulbs—it could happen anywhere in the house at any time, no matter what size bulb we installed. The combination of an ordinary light bulb and this extraordinary current was consistently devastating.

Likewise, Jesus' mind and body were connected to a heart that was so full of love that it regularly sent enormous surges of sorrow throughout His system and at any time could create a deadly overload of grief. A person's love for others can result in great joy, but it can also produce enormous amounts of pain. The greater the love, the greater the hurt. Isaiah called Jesus Wonderful Counselor, Mighty God, Everlasting Father, the Prince of Peace (see Isaiah 9:6). But the prophet manifested one of his deepest insights into Jesus' identity when he spoke of Him as a Man of Sorrows and acquainted with grief (see Isaiah 53:3).

"How few have any conception of the anguish that rent the heart of the Son of God during His thirty years of life upon the earth. The path from the manger to Calvary was shadowed by sorrow and grief. He was the man of sorrow, and *endured such heartache as no human language can portray.*"[1]

Christ also had a much greater capacity for experiencing mental and emotional pain than we do. Even the most large-hearted bearer of hurt among us falls far short of what our Lord endured. I may have a teaspoon-sized capacity for empathizing with people's pain. But Christ apparently had the unique and awful ability to feel others' hurt and sorrow by the ton. The grief He felt differed from ours in both its amazing quantity and its white-hot intensity.[2]

The effects of sin permeated every nook and cranny of life on earth to an extraordinary degree, and Jesus often shed bitter tears as He contemplated the woe of the world.

1. Nature

Jesus sorrowed over what sin had done to His precious creation. The animal kingdom, once a vivid illustration of cooperation and peaceful relationships in Eden, was now reduced to "survival of the fittest." Lions and tigers tore apart smaller animals. Vultures lived off rotting carcasses. Most of nature, from snakes to eagles, lived by killing. Whole species developed specialized ways of poisoning and capturing their prey. Christ's sensitive heart beat in harmony with that of His Father, who cared about the death of even a tiny sparrow (see Matthew 10:29).

Sin brought decay and blight to the plant kingdom as well. Thorns and briars appeared on the same stems as the most delicate flowers. Lush landscapes were reduced to wastelands. The Son of God surveyed it all and wept.

As a boy, several of my summers were spent at day camp, relishing the nature stories and crafts. At registration for classes one year, I ran my finger down the list of printed possibilities and found woodworking, last on the list but first in my interests. The teacher and I decided that I would make a paddle boat, complete with an elastic band that gave it the ability to navigate real waters. I spent every spare minute sawing, planing, measuring, hammering, and sanding, day after day. The thing became a labor of love. My goal was to unveil it grandly when Mom and Dad came to inspect our productions on the final day of camp.

Eventually the boat was finished and needed only a test run the day before the parents were to arrive. As it turned out, I was sick that day and had to stay home but felt confident, nonetheless. At last the moment arrived when I escorted my dad by the hand into the work area, beaming. I looked along the shelf for the special place I had carefully dry-docked my cherished creation, but the spot was empty. The boat had vanished! A sense of panic came over me. As I turned, I looked into the outstretched hands of the instructor cradling the broken remnants of my little vessel. Sadly he explained that the day before some boys had sailed it roughly without permission. My dad held me as I sobbed. It was a lot of hurt for a little boy.

My wife is from Yugoslavia, where as a teenager she had entered several national writing contests in school and won awards. When she moved to America, her struggles with a new language created an insecurity that halted any further attempts at prose. Much later, after eight years of marriage, I finally coaxed her to resurrect her dormant gift. With a pen in one hand and a dictionary for double-checking in the other, she carefully composed a sensitive essay on motherhood for a newsletter for ministers' wives. After one more round of self-doubt and reassurance, my wife managed a hopeful smile as she mailed the article to the editor who had requested it in the first place.

When our copy of the newsletter arrived, my wife scanned it eagerly. They hadn't printed her article! We checked again the next month, but nothing. After three issues, she assumed it hadn't been good enough and asked the editor if she would return it, for sentimental reasons. The woman then confessed that her composition had been accepted, but before they could print it, in the clutter of a basement office, it had been lost, irretrievably lost. My wife told her, "Oh, that's OK." But it wasn't OK. She hasn't written an essay since.

It hurts deeply to see something you have created and poured so much love into in any way damaged, or worse, destroyed. Jesus felt a similar, yet far deeper, hurt over the demise of His own once pristine creation.

2. Human diseases

If Jesus ached over the havoc sin had wrought in the natural world, imagine His anguish over its appalling effects on humanity, the crowning work of creation, made in the very image of God!

"Our world is a vast lazar house [a place filled with loathsome diseases], a scene of misery that we dare not allow even our thoughts to dwell upon. Did we realize it as it is, the burden would be too terrible. *Yet God feels it all.*"[3]

While on earth, Christ sorrowed over the cruel illnesses—past, present, and future—that ruined the lives of millions.[4] Leprosy, paralysis, heart disease, deformities, today's crack babies, and on and on. So many of His earthly children were fevered and stricken. No one was ever supposed to utter the words "I am sick." There were never supposed to be ambulances, hospitals, or hospice shelters. Families were never supposed to stand around the beds of loved ones and wrestle with the awful decision of whether or not to keep them breathing on a respirator. Children were never supposed to shuffle along cancer wards with bald heads and sunken eyes. Our bodies were designed to live forever in undiminished vigor and perfect health. Only Jesus knew how terribly the plan had been marred. Only He could feel the hurt to the very depths of His being.

3. Human relationships

Christ also suffered as He contemplated evil's devastating impact on the relationships between people. Sin's poisonous effect on human relationships is dramatically revealed in the experience of Adam and Eve. Prior to sin, earth's first couple lived in unblemished, untarnished harmony. They cherished one another and shared a warm, intimate relationship with God. Only minutes after they sinned, however, their attitudes, values, motives, and self-image changed completely. It is one of the most amazing "Dr. Jekyll and Mr. Hyde" stories of history.

Suddenly fear, guilt, selfishness, and blame dominated. The two ran and hid from the One who made them, the One who had filled their lives with joy. Asked about his sin, Adam blamed his wife. "It's that woman you saddled me with, she deceived me. It's all her fault."

Eve then pinned the blame on the serpent and, in effect, on God Himself. "It's that snake You made. You never should have let that creature into this garden anyway!"

Our earthly culture is now so thoroughly infected with selfishness and sin that we have become callused to how incredibly abnormal our world really is. In heaven, if someone told a tiny white lie about their neighbor, it would make banner headlines. The *Heaven's Daily* newspaper would scream in ten-inch bold letters, "Man Gossips!" Unfallen beings throughout the universe would react with dread and amazement at the awful news. We could envision reporters encamped on the offender's lawn, waiting for the latest update.

Here on earth such a sin would go totally unnoticed. We even chuckle at the very thought of a newspaper reporting such a trivial incident. To use ten-inch letters, our own newspapers have to read, "World War Declared!"

Imagine trying to tell a fish how wonderful it is to live on dry land and breathe real fresh air. "What is that stuff about flower-strewn valleys and snow-capped mountains?" the fish inquires. "And as for your description of furry animals with four feet . . . I just don't get it." Land is a totally foreign world. The sea is all that a tuna knows!

In a way the fish is you or I, immersed in a world where living with the effects of sin has become the norm. We swim in it all the time. Our lives are awash in abnormal happenings, at least from heaven's point of view. Trying to imagine a land or a culture where perfect, unconditional love is all that people know is extremely difficult.

Yet those hard-to-comprehend heavenly values and attitudes were alive and well within the heart of Christ. Perfect love beat within His chest. That was the unsullied perspective out of which He viewed the world. Jesus never became callused to sin; He never adjusted.

I am allergic to, of all things, Brazil nuts. My first encounter with these predatory nuts came when I was about ten and our family visited relatives for Thanksgiving. The meal took longer to prepare than planned, and my kindly aunt passed around a box of scrumptious looking chocolates to quiet our complaints. I gulped one with a particularly creative squiggle on top, and within minutes my throat began to close. Frightened, I ran into the kitchen, pointing to my neck and wheezing a pathetic plea. Thankfully my physician uncle had the proper antidote on hand. Nonetheless, I spent most of the day flat on my back without a single bite of my favorite blueberry pie. Now, whenever I eat at someone's home, I have to give my standard speech: "I'm sorry, but I'm really allergic to this certain kind of nut . . ." Frustrating, but necessary.

Similarly, Jesus was allergic to the impact of sin on those around Him. Contact with human brokenness caused an intense reaction within Him. Ellen White tells us, "As the sinless One, His nature *recoiled from* evil. He endured struggles and torture of soul, in a world of sin."[5] His inner spirit cringed in the presence of evil as we might at the sound of fingernails scraping across a blackboard, only far worse. "Would that we could comprehend the significance of the words, 'Christ suffered, being tempted.' [See Hebrews 2:18.] While he was free from the taint of sin, the refined sensibilities of his holy nature *rendered contact with evil unspeakably painful to him.*"[6]

The Spirit of Prophecy indicates that "Every sin, every discord, every defiling lust that transgression had brought, *was torture to His spirit.*"[7] He was tortured by *discord*. That word covers not only our big fights but also all the little dissonances and fractures, the tiny stresses and strains, that creep into everyday relationships. Now imagine taking someone with that sensitivity, that degree of caring, and making him grow up in the sin-infected town of Nazareth. As Christ walked the streets of His discordant hometown and heard a customer scold a shopkeeper, or husband and wife exchange mean, hurtful words, His heart was pierced. He suffered over the animosity between the Jews and Rome, plus all the other countless cruelties in society. Ellen White resorts to the extremes of human language to describe Jesus' pain: "Christ *mourned* for the transgression of every human being."[8]

As Isaiah wrote, "In all their affliction He was afflicted" (Isaiah 63:9, KJV). I can watch the 6:00 A.M. news and hear about robberies, murders, riots, muggings, battles, and murmur with detachment, "What a shame," and forget it. But not Christ. For Him it would be anguishing to view. These are His kids, His children, His own creation self-destructing on sin!

"The sorrow and anguish of the Son of God for the sins of the world were proportionate to His divine excellence and purity, as well as to the magnitude of the offense."[9] A musician with perfect pitch suffers far more at the sound of a severely out-of-tune instrument than does someone with a tin ear. A profoundly skilled architect sorrows over the bombing of a great cathedral far more than one who has no appreciation for the time and talent it took to build it. As the universe's supreme expert on love, Jesus could see the full contrast between good and evil, and it pained Him far more than we can imagine.

4. The lost

Without question, Christ experienced the greatest, most heart-wrenching sorrow over those who refused to be converted and give their lives to God. Millions were dying without hope of eternal life. Jesus would never see them again except on the terrible, heartbreaking day of judgment. The following tragic story illustrates the kind of pain He felt over the lost, every single day.

On March 19, 1979, Stephanie Ambrose May lost in one horrific plane crash:

- *her husband,* John Edward May, 51, chief executive officer and chairman of the board of May petroleum;
- *her only son,* David Edward May, 22, a senior at the University of Texas;
- *her daughter,* Karla Emily May, 18, a senior at Highland Park High School;
- *her son-in-law,* Richard Owen Snyder, 27, landman for the R. L. Burns Corp.

This woman's grief was mingled with hope because her family members were Christians. Nonetheless, she lived everyone's worst nightmare. Her agonized lament provides a glimpse into what Jesus felt as He mourned over those who died without hope and without God. Her grief over temporary death can dimly illustrate His grief over death that was eternal. She writes:

"Late afternoon—doorbell— . . . the awesome news of tragedy—(death, plus death, plus death, plus death = death).

"Down, down into the depths of depths in hollow, dark desolation . . . I scream in my empty space—my loves, my loves of life . . . The tearing away— the deep loss of all I have lived for and loved—my family, oh God, why my family?

"I loved them each and every one to the fullest of my capacity . . .

"I am crushed, broken, and stripped naked . . . engulfed in tragedy and wrapped in a blanket of pain.

"Again I pray, again I cry, for from the bare, darkest corridors of my mind and body, I tear at the darkness and grasp for Your light. Release me from the erupting volcanic bowels of this earth's hell. Leave me not on the barren, cold, craggy, mountainous peaks.

"I yearn for [their] clasping hand, a wink, a smile. . . . Tears of anguish, tears of pain."[10]

Every day, Christ suffered a sense of loss far greater than this dear mother's devastating grief. All around Jesus, thousands of His children were choosing eternal death, placing themselves just beyond the reach of His yearning, saving love. He cared for each one as if they were the only one, and it wrung His heart whenever someone averted their eyes and turned away. For Him, just to get out of bed and face each new day took a heroic effort.

Once we realize the inner pain that regularly burdened His soul, we can more fully appreciate what an absolute miracle it was that He consistently ex- uded such life and joy! It was heaven to be in His presence. No morbid expres- sion dominated His countenance. He did not shuffle along the street in discour- agement. Little children would not have been attracted to a sourpuss. Kids are impeccable judges of character, and they flocked to Him in droves. They loved to climb up on His lap, stroke His beard, and listen to His stories. This is the same Man who said, " 'I am come that they might have life, and that they might have it more abundantly' " (John 10:10, KJV). He declared, " 'These things have I spoken unto you, that my joy might remain in you, and that your joy might be full' " (John 15:11, KJV).

One of my daughter's best friends in academy was class president two years in a row. That upbeat young woman tackled her many responsibilities with opti- mism and energy, obtained excellent grades, and gained a reputation for helping others. Yet few people knew that she suffered from an almost constant, nauseat- ing form of migraine headaches. Neither would those who came in contact with Jesus have imagined the underlying hurt that tore at His heart. He rose above it all through spending enormous amounts of time in prayer. Mark's record is very typical: "And in the morning, a great while before day, he rose and went out to a lonely place, and there he prayed" (Mark 1:35). The following comment underscores Mark's words: "He required all the divine support and comfort which His Father was ready to impart to His Son. . . . Christ found joy and comfort in communion with His Father. Here He could unburden His sorrows that were crushing Him."[11] "Through continual communion He received life from God, that He might impart life to the world."[12]

Because of Jesus' acute sensitivity to sin, it was imperative that He periodically get away in order to maintain His sanity. The Father had to shield Christ from too intense and prolonged an exposure to the work of sin or else His profound sorrow over its effects would have broken Him.

There are a number of children who have a rare, extreme sensitivity to light from the sun, as well as other forms of ultraviolet light. The parents of one little girl didn't realize what was causing her face, arms, and legs to break out in terrible ulcerous sores and blisters. Unfortunately, they loved camping and took her on many summer trips and hikes before the doctors pinpointed her disease. Today she is quite disfigured. The illness is called erythropoietic protoporphyria. These unfortunate children have to sleep all day and play outside only at night. Their highly unusual reaction to light makes it essential that they avoid exposure to its potentially lethal rays.[13]

Christ suffered from a similar sensitivity, except in His case He experienced an acute reaction to the lost condition of humankind. The enormity of His love made Him hypersensitive to the spiritually ruinous effects of sin.

At times His sorrow was so deep that it could not be soothed, and it poured forth in torrents. Just before He raised Lazarus from the dead, "Jesus wept" (John 11:35). "It was not only because of the scene before Him that Christ wept. The weight of the grief of ages was upon Him. He saw the terrible effects of the transgression of God's law. . . . His heart was pierced with the pain of the human family of all ages and in all lands. The woes of the sinful race were heavy upon His soul, and the fountain of His tears was broken up as He longed to relieve all their distress."[14]

Not many days later, on the Sunday before Jesus died, the Savior's triumphal procession halted on a hill overlooking the magnificent but doomed city of Jerusalem. From His kingly position on the back of a donkey, Christ surveyed the scene before Him. The shouts of joy and victory from thousands of supporters soon dwindled to an anxious hush.

The gospel writer Luke then tells us, "And when he drew near and saw the city he wept over it" (Luke 19:41). The word *wept* "does not mean merely that tears forced themselves up and fell down His face. It suggests rather the heaving of the bosom, and the sob and cry of a soul in agony. We could have no stronger word than the word that is used there."[15] The prophet Hosea captured the Savior's feelings on that Palm Sunday when he wrote, "Ephraim, how could I part with you? Israel, how could I give you up? . . . My heart recoils from it, my whole being trembles at the thought" (Hosea 11:8, Jerusalem). One person is worth worlds, but here was an entire nation that would be lost! Note carefully this striking description of the scene: The throng of celebrants is "surprised and disappointed to see His eyes fill with tears, and His *body rock to and fro* like a tree before the tempest, while a *wail of anguish bursts from His quivering lips. . . .* [Christ is] in an agony of tears."[16]

Certainly Christ's sorrow over the city of Jerusalem was extraordinary, but it was actually mild compared to what awaited Him in Gethsemane. As Jesus entered the garden, He described His own grief with the startling words, " 'My soul is exceeding sorrowful, even unto death' " (Matthew 26:38, KJV). Upon arriving in Gethsemane, Jesus' angel guard was removed, and for the first time God the Father allowed that which He had heretofore carefully prevented. Hundreds of evil angels were now given complete access to Christ, and they pressed in around Him like wolves. Their purpose was to take advantage of His astonishing sorrow over man's self-destruction. In an attempt to discourage Christ from going to the cross, the evil angels rehearsed to Him the hopeless condition of humankind. Name after name, they went down the list of those who had rejected God.

"The hosts of darkness are there to make sin appear as extensive, deep, and horrible as possible. . . . The working of the vigilant foe in presenting to Christ the *vast proportions of transgression*, caused such poignant pain that He felt He could not remain in the immediate presence of any human being. He could not bear that even His disciples should witness His agony as He contemplated the woe of the world."[17] "The suffering Son of God leaves His disciples, for the power of darkness *rushes upon Him with an irresistible force* which bows Him to the earth."[18]

In hopes that Jesus would acknowledge the unrelenting hold that evil had on humanity and admit to the futility of the cross, Satan's forces dwelt on every tragic, grisly page in the catalogue of sin.

"Billions of angels have already rebelled against you. Your own nation has rejected you, and your very disciples will forsake you. Countless human beings will be captivated and ruined," they snarled.

The spiritual obituary of unnumbered multitudes was accentuated. The loss of just one person would have been a crushing blow, but the loss was multiplied by millions! Name by precious name—Ruth . . . Henry . . . Robert . . . Jane . . . Frank . . . Sally. Story after tragic story. "They don't want you, Jesus. You're dying for nothing, Jesus," they continued. "They're not interested in your redemption! It's all a waste!"

The effect on Christ was murderous. His breathing came in gasps. He collapsed to the earth and shuddered before the catastrophe of sin. As Isaiah rightly predicted, "Surely he hath borne our griefs, and carried our sorrows" (Isaiah 53:4, KJV). "He was overwhelmed with horror and consternation at the fearful work sin had wrought."[19] Agony beyond the endurance of human flesh drained His life forces. Quickly the angel Gabriel came to offer encouragement and delay the execution of Jesus' spirit.

After only a few brief hours' reprieve, however, the same traumatic scene was repeated on Calvary. We are given the following important insight: "And now the Lord of glory was dying, a ransom for the race . . . It was not the dread of death that weighed upon Him . . . *His suffering was from a sense of the malignity of sin*, a knowledge that through familiarity with evil, man had become blinded to its enormity. *Christ saw how deep is the hold of sin upon the human heart*, how few would be willing to break from its power . . . He saw multitudes perishing within reach of abundant help."[20] The Son of God was again overwhelmed with the horrifying results of evil.

The devil hurled against Christ all the demons of hell. Excruciating mental and emotional pain surged through Jesus' heart and mind. Grief deeper and more terrible than we can know overwhelmed His humanity. This time no angel assistance was offered, Satan pressed too far, and the Son of God bowed His head and died. His great, loving heart burst, in no small part from sorrow over the pain of our own self-destruction.

As we discern the intensity of Jesus' pain over the effects of sin, we can begin to comprehend Ellen White's statements regarding the full dimensions of the Trinity's woe. She writes, "Those who think of the result of hastening or hindering the gospel think of it in relation to themselves and to the world. Few give thought to the suffering that sin has caused our Creator. . . . *The cross is a revelation to our dull senses of the pain that, from its very inception, sin has brought to the heart of God*."[21] In the killer sorrow Christ experienced at Gethsemane and on the cross, we see a demonstration of what the entire Godhead has felt every day since sin entered the universe. They care that much. They long to save us that much.

The pain the human family has endured from evil is certainly immense, but that cannot hold a candle to the agony of the Trinity. The book of Revelation teaches that after sin has been destroyed "there shall be no more death, neither sorrow, nor crying, neither shall there be any more pain: for the former things are passed away" (Revelation 21:4, KJV). No one looks forward to that wonderful time more earnestly than God.

1. Ellen G. White, *Advent Review and Sabbath Herald,* 20 Dec. 1892, italics supplied.
2. Ellen G. White, *That I May Know Him* (Hagerstown, Md.: Review and Herald, 1964), 64.
3. Ellen G. White, *Education* (Nampa, Idaho: Pacific Press®, 1952), 264, italics supplied.
4. *Confrontation,* 36, 51.
5. Ellen G. White, *Steps to Christ* (Nampa, Idaho: Pacific Press®, n.d.), 93, 94, italics supplied.
6. *Advent Review and Sabbath Herald,* 8 Nov. 1887, italics supplied.
7. *The Desire of Ages,* 111, italics supplied.
8. *Advent Review and Sabbath Herald*, 12 June 1900.
9. *Confrontation,* 50.
10. B. Clayton Bell, "A Look at Grief," *Leadership*, (Fall 1980): 43-46.
11. Ellen G. White, *Testimonies to the Church* (Nampa, Idaho: Pacific Press®, 1948), 2:202.
12. *That I May Know Him,* 259.
13. *The Merck Manual of Medical Information* (Whitehouse Station, N.J.: Merck Research Laboratories, 1997), 690.
14. *The Desire of Ages,* 534.
15. Norval Geldenhuys, *Commentary on the Gospel of Luke: The New International Commentary on the New Testament,* 484.
16. *The Desire of Ages,* 575.
17. Ellen G. White, MS 35, 1895.
18. *The Sufferings of Christ,* 19.
19. Ibid., 23.
20. *The Desire of Ages,* 752, 753.
21. *Education,* 263.

Chapter 8

Forsaken

The speaker's topic for Thursday morning college chapel was, "From Communism to Christ." After opening announcements, three draggy hymns and prayer, a five-foot four-inch, brown-haired, attractive Yugoslavian coed in a blue dress stepped to the podium and shared her conversion story. I put down my *Time* magazine, leaned forward, and listened intently.

That evening I phoned her dorm. "Is Ann there? Ann Zuvicic?" When she answered, I launched into what I thought was a very clever opener. "Hi. We've just taken a survey to determine the prettiest girl on campus, and guess what . . . you won! Would you like to go out on a date with me this Saturday evening?"

Corny, but effective. Last Christmas we celebrated our twenty-sixth wedding anniversary and are more in love than ever. Love stories between human beings have been the stuff of countless books, articles, and films ever since cupid shot his first arrow.

But the greatest love story ever told does not involve humanity at all. The most compelling, the most intense, love story in the entire universe is the love the members of the Godhead have had for each other from all eternity. If we put together all of the caring and kindness shown by humans all over the globe since the beginning of Creation, it would be as only a thimbleful of water compared to the ocean of love the members of the Trinity feel, moment by moment, for one another.

We are so earth-centered in our thinking we tend to forget that human beings, and indeed all created beings, are relative newcomers on the scene of life.
The Godhead does not "need" us in order to be fulfilled. The Father, Son, and
Holy Spirit have experienced infinitely complete joy and delight in their shared
life for unlimited trillions and trillions and trillions of years. And what a perfect
union that must be! Each member of the Trinity is defined by love that is unconditional, constant, and without limit. Only they can fully appreciate one another.
Only they can fully communicate together.

After having been so unimaginably inseparable, it was at Gethsemane and
Golgotha that the unthinkable happened within the Godhead. The intimate bond
between Jesus and the Father was severed, causing Christ to ultimately utter that
awful, bloodcurdling cry, " 'My God, my God, why hast thou forsaken me?' "
(Matthew 27:46, KJV). Separation from His Father was the pain Jesus dreaded
most, the pain that finally crushed Him.

Jesus' concept of God as a loving heavenly Father came particularly from
His relationship with Joseph. It is unfortunate that Joseph's influence on Christ
has received such scant attention. After all, the divine call came to a parenting
team.

One can imagine Joseph holding Baby Jesus on his knee and singing lulla-
bies or telling Bible stories, perhaps even at times acting them out. The little
boy's first prayers probably included pieces of phrases learned from Joseph.
Periodically you might have seen Christ perched happily on Joseph's shoulders
on their way to the sea, where two rugged arms supported the lad in His first
swimming lessons, and a confident, husky voice kept repeating, "Trust me, I'll
hold you up!"

When Joseph came to tuck Jesus into bed, he might occasionally have found
Him either in tears or strangely quiet after a day of being ridiculed. He would
have done his best to bring comfort and assurance by putting his face right next
to the Boy Jesus and whispering, "You're one great kid, and I love you, more
than ever."

In the carpenter's shop one could see Joseph's hands on top of Christ's as the
little boy tried some tool for the very first time. They probably hiked up often
into the hills together to cut timber and would wind up sitting on an overhang
chewing on some straw and talking about a boy's interests and dreams. As Christ
grew into the teens, Joseph gave Him more responsibility at a building site, such
as measuring out the floor plan or cutting in a critical corner, all under Dad's
patient and skillful eye.

During those formative years, Joseph and Mary must have thrilled to teach

Jesus about His miraculous birth and His real Father in heaven. After evening worship, Christ often looked long into the starry night. He poured over the Scriptures as one would letters from home, searching for self-understanding.

His happiest moments were the hours between waking and breakfast when He could talk and sing to the Father in some secluded spot and strain to catch the whisperings of each treasured reply. At times He might have climbed His favorite tree, the tallest, just to feel as near to the Father as possible. At age twelve, this special relationship was so central to His life that He appealed to it as the most natural reason in the world for missing His ride back home from Jerusalem. " 'Did you not know that I must be about My Father's business?' " (Luke 2:49).

Later, during His public ministry, Jesus repeatedly spoke of His intimate bond with the Father.

1. *He and God the Father loved each other intimately:*
   • " 'Therefore doth my Father love me' " (John 10:17).
   • " 'I love the Father' " (John 14: 31).
2. *Jesus derived His very life from the Father:*
   • " 'The living Father hath sent me, and I live by the Father' " (John 6:57).
3. *The Father taught Jesus what to say:*
   • " 'I do nothing of myself; but as my Father hath taught me, I speak these things' " (John 8:28).
4. *The Father enabled Christ to minister to others:*
   • " 'The Father that dwelleth in me, he doeth the works' " (John 14:10).
5. *Jesus and God the Father were completely inseparable:*
   • " 'I and my Father are one' " (John 10:30).

It was only because of His connection with God that Christ survived the relentless torrent of hate, criticism, and abuse that beat against Him from His earliest days. Intimate communion with God was as natural and necessary to Him as breathing. In order to function and cope, "Jesus sought earnestly for strength from his Father. He regarded communication with God more essential than his daily food."[1]

The Savior's relationship to heaven was like a deep-sea diver who works in a foreign and potentially lethal environment but is connected to the life-giving source of oxygen above. The crushing weight of responsibility for the salvation of the world and the need to be absolutely perfect every moment of every day necessitated an extraordinary bond between Christ and the Father.

As their unity grew in intensity, so however, did the haunting reality that one day they would be separated. For the first time in eternity, that closeness would be ripped apart for the sake of an earthful of callous rebels. *Jesus, however, never planned on being separated from His heavenly Father forever.* In the plan of salvation that the Trinity had worked out thousands of years before, the separation would be excruciating, but at least it would be temporary. It would occur twice, once in Gethsemane, and then again on the cross. After that the Savior would rise from the tomb early Sunday morning.

Nonetheless, the prospect of even those short-lived separations caused Christ to shudder. It would be by far the most agonizing experience of His entire earthly life. He periodically awoke suddenly during the middle of the night, wide-eyed, bathed in a cold sweat, as the upcoming trauma intruded upon His sleep.

You see, sometimes knowing the future can be a blessing, but it can also be a terrible curse. How far ahead of time would you like to know that you will be in a horrendous car crash and suffer third-degree burns over 80 percent of your body? A few days in advance? Several months? How would that foreknowledge affect your living? Jesus knew about His appointment with the fiery pain of separation for years.

As the dreaded hour drew near, Christ's inner turmoil increased significantly. On the Tuesday before His crucifixion, He paused to contemplate the upcoming isolation from His Father and declared, " 'Now is my soul troubled' " (John 12:27). The Son of God experienced intensely dark feelings at that time:

"In anticipation, Christ was already drinking the cup of bitterness. His humanity shrank from the hour of abandonment, when to all appearance He would be deserted even by God. . . . A foreboding of . . . the Father's wrath because of sin caused the spirit of Jesus to faint, and the *pallor of death to overspread His countenance.*"[2]

Despite the impending nightmarish separation, our Lord was able to focus on the issues at hand during the remainder of Passion Week with remarkable clarity, deliberateness, and poise. Each night He spent hour after hour in prayer, finding the strength to live above the anxiety that clawed at His soul. His positive, uplifting attitude at the Last Supper on Thursday evening was particularly remarkable considering that Gethsemane was now less than two or three hours away. Speaking with great personal affection and rock-solid assurance, Christ looked lovingly into the eyes of His soon-to-be-scattered disciples and told them,

" 'Let not your heart be troubled: ye believe in God, believe also in me. In my Father's house are many mansions: if it were not so, I would have told you. I go to prepare a place for you. And if I go and prepare a place for you, I will come

again, and receive you unto myself; that where I am, there ye may be also' "
(John 14:1).

Just as He left the upper room, Jesus even led the little band in a song of
praise, the familiar Passover Hallel from Psalm 117 (KJV):

> O praise the Lord, all ye nations:
> Praise Him, all ye people.
> For his merciful kindness is great toward us:
> And the truth of the Lord endureth for ever.
> Praise ye the Lord.[3]

After the Last Supper, they filed out through the southeast gate of the city
and began the slow, winding descent to the Kidron Valley, about two hundred
feet below. Within sight now of Gethsemane, Christ talked earnestly with His
disciples. The full moon illuminated the fateful night and revealed a mature
grapevine overhanging the path. Jesus held a lush cluster of grapes in His outstretched hand and said, " 'I am the vine; you are the branches' " (John 15:1,
NIV). A little farther on He stopped, lifted His eyes toward heaven, and prayed,
"Holy Father, keep them in thy name, which thou hast given me, that they may
be one, even as we are one. . . . Now I am coming to thee; and these things I
speak in the world, that they may have my joy fulfilled in themselves" (John
17:11, 13). Inspiring, courageous words, spoken in the confidence of the presence of God.

Within only a few steps, however, the scene changed dramatically. From
calm assurance and optimism, He suddenly plunged into gut-wrenching difficulty. The contrast is startling. Spiritually and emotionally, it was as if Jesus
stepped under the flow of a four-hundred-foot waterfall and was shoved, flailing
and gasping, far below the surface of the river.

The Gospel writer Mark observes, "And he [Christ] took with him Peter and
James and John, and *began to be greatly distressed and troubled"* (Mark 14:33,
italics supplied). One of the Greek words used here can also mean "to be terrified."[4] He came face to face with something He personally found extremely
frightening.

Jesus then uttered the startling words, "My soul is exceeding sorrowful,
even unto death" (Matthew 26:38, KJV). Here was a sorrow so acute, so poisonous, it could kill. The separation from His Father that haunted His thinking for
years was now becoming stark reality. As our sins were laid upon the Savior as
our Substitute, He sensed the Father pulling away and was instantly overwhelmed

with heart-pounding, paralyzing grief.

"His form swayed as if He were about to fall. . . . Every step that He now took was with labored effort. He groaned aloud, as if suffering under the pressure of a terrible burden. Twice His companions supported Him or He would have fallen to the earth."[5]

Christ left the disciples and stumbled a short distance to a small clearing before collapsing under a tall cypress tree. He lay prostrate, face down on the cold, familiar ground and dug His fingers into the earth in an attempt to grasp something stable, something immovable, in the dizzying spiritual descent. "He felt that by sin He was being separated from His Father. The gulf was so broad, so black, so deep, that His spirit shuddered before it."[6]

As I grope for some small point of connection with Jesus' pain, some tiny link of personal understanding, I recall the time as a boy when separation tore at my own tender, unsuspecting heart. I loved my mom very much, but circumstances made my affection for my dad particularly intense. Dad could fix anything. Every weekend he and I tackled a waiting line of projects. The man who had been a decorated soldier during WWII became a little boy's hero.

My parents struggled through chronic marital difficulties. Over the years, their arguments grew more frequent and hurtful. One afternoon, another heated conflict, worse than usual, sent Dad storming upstairs. From the hallway below I could hear dresser drawers being opened hastily and clothes hangers in the corner closet banging from side to side. A nervous shiver ran through my body.

Suddenly Dad appeared at the top of the stairs with a suitcase in each hand. As he stomped deliberately down the steps, my mind raced for words to blurt out an innocent plea that would stop this nightmare. Surely Dad would fix this too! In the hall, he paused and hugged me tightly. My desperate speech stuck in my throat. I sobbed and clutched at his tan jacket. Then in a blur Dad was gone! In dismay, I peered out a nearby window through a prism of tears as the dark blue Chevy we had worked on so often pulled away from the yard, stealing a best friend and leaving behind a fearful, heart-broken little boy.

With an infinitely greater sense of loss, Christ felt His own beloved Father withdrawing. With hot tears and quivering lips He pleaded, "Please, please, if there is any other way!" For an hour He prayed in agony. I can imagine Him crying out in anguish, "My Father, the time has come. From eternity We have been One. You are My life. We have never been apart, never. How can I endure it? The shame of crucifixion, the pain of the nails . . . My mind abhors it all, every ounce of it. But what is that compared to being separated from You? How will I survive?

"Even now I can feel the change between Us. I can sense You drawing back. The distance is already more than I can bear. Can you still hear my cries? Are you watching over Me still? The devil is swallowing me up with temptation. The pounding in my head. My heart is going to leap out of My chest. It is so hard to breathe. The fear and uncertainty. There is so much at stake. I love You, Father. Don't go any farther away! No! Father, don't draw back. It is already so dark, so distant. O Father!"

The Son of God was in anguish, and the very foundations of the universe trembled. The Spirit of Prophecy tells us that *"Christ was amazed* with the horror of darkness which enclosed Him."[7] Most experiences in life are worse in anticipation than they are in reality. This was just the opposite. With His brilliant mind and uncanny insight, the Savior had undoubtedly tried to imagine this crucial moment over and over again during His ministry. Yet even He vastly underestimated the situation. Even He was stunned at how overwhelming the separation in the garden turned out to be. The situation was far worse than His most nightmarish expectations.

As if that experience was not hard enough, two additional terrors now inserted themselves into Jesus' mind. *First,* Christ was afraid that in His humanity He would not be able to endure. The Incarnation handed Him a mind and body that bore but faint resemblance to the ideal, powerful frame inhabited by Adam before the fall. Several thousand years of sin had taken an enormous toll on humankind's mental abilities and physical stamina. Christ entered the arena with a greatly diminished capacity to survive. *Second,* the Saviour was tempted to think that this temporary separation from God would, in fact, become eternal! The devil and his legions pressed in like wolves and bowed Jesus to the earth with the shattering claim that if He chose to continue, He would in fact be saying Goodbye to God, not for a few hours but *forever.*

"With the issues of the conflict before Him, Christ's soul was filled with dread of separation from God. Satan told him that if He became the surety for a sinful world, the separation would be eternal. He would be identified with Satan's kingdom, and would *nevermore be one with God.*"[8]

Eternal separation was unthinkable, yet the devil built an ingenious and compelling case. The supernatural forces of evil "well-nigh overpower[ed] Him."[9] Longing for some word of encouragement, the Savior raised Himself painfully from the ground and staggered back to the disciples. His agony so contorted His features that when He wakened His three closest followers *they hardly recognized Him!*[10] Addressing Peter in particular, Jesus spoke in a hoarse, labored voice, "Please, could you not pray for one hour?"

Feeling faint, He stumbled back to the place of suffering, where His torment intensified as the devil pressed harder still. "Now His voice was heard on the still evening air . . . *full of human anguish.*"[11] Jesus' heart pounded, and His breathing came in shallow gasps. Wails of sorrow broke upon the quiet evening in loud, woeful sobs. His skin turned cold and clammy to the touch. Overcome with nausea, He vomited the Passover meal then doubled over in racking dry heaves. Tears poured from His reddened eyes, forming narrow rivulets down His soil-stained cheeks. Blood oozed from numerous pores as if to escape the torment within. Twice more He pleaded with the Father to find some other way, but submitted, as He had done all His life, to Heaven's will.

The separation struggle soon depleted Christ's life forces. The gray-green, shadow-etched scene around Him began to narrow in His vision. As our Lord neared unconsciousness, He crumpled as a dead man onto the dew-laden ground. Heaven immediately dispatched the angel Gabriel to revive the intrepid Sufferer. He cradled the Savior's head in his strong arm, wiped His hot forehead, then pointed toward heaven while speaking words of comfort, assurance, and hope.[12] With remarkable stamina and courage, Jesus eventually recovered sufficiently to somehow carry on. *The first separation was over.* With the sense of His Father's presence restored, Christ went forth to confront His betrayer.

Throughout the ensuing arrest, trials, beatings, scourgings, and the first three hours of the crucifixion, Christ was once again confident, assured, and conscious of the Father's presence. The sense of separation was removed. During the morning hours on the cross, He could confidently assure the thief next to Him that they would both be in paradise.

By midday on Friday, however, all that changed. *At Calvary He again experienced the same kind of separation He endured in Gethsemane, only worse.* For approxmiately three hours, between noon and 3:00 P.M., He again felt deserted by His Father, abandoned, and utterly alone.[13]

Each second that passed on Golgotha felt like an eternity. The Savior's eyes fell upon two figures in the distance hurrying along the highway—a father with his arm around his son—and tears streamed down Jesus' face. He scanned the distant heavens as His mind replayed scenes from His own childhood—the special place where He prayed; the temple visits; the tree He climbed to get as near to the Father as possible. The sense of loss and the weight of grief were unbearable.

In his book *Night*, Elie Wiesel recounts a time of nightmarish separation during the Holocaust. In stark detail he recalls the moment he and his own father faced apparently permanent separation from each other in a Nazi concentration camp.

"Not far from us, flames were leaping up from a ditch, gigantic flames. They were burning something. A lorry drew up at the pit and delivered its load— little children. . . . I pinched my face. Was I still alive? Was I awake? I could not believe it. How could it be possible for them to burn people, children. . . . My father's voice drew me from my thoughts. . . . His voice was terribly sad. I realized that he did not want to see . . . the burning of his only son.

"My forehead was bathed in cold sweat.

"[My father] was weeping. His body was shaken convulsively.

"We continued our march. We were gradually drawing closer to the ditch, from which an infernal heat was rising. . . . Our line had now only fifteen paces to cover. I bit my lips so that my father would not hear my teeth chattering. Ten steps still. Eight. Seven. We marched slowly on, as though following a hearse at our own funeral. Four steps more. Three steps. There it is now, right in front of us, the pit and its flames. . . . In the depths of my heart, I bade farewell to my father, to the whole universe. . . . The moment had come. I was face to face with the Angel of Death.

"No. Two steps from the pit we were ordered to turn to the left and made to go into a barracks.

"I pressed my father's hand."[14]

At Calvary Christ felt His Father's grip loosen, and He continued on alone into the inferno. Separation again became a reality, and Jesus began to burn.

For three momentous hours after noontime the entire region was miraculously plunged into thick, pitch-black darkness, symbolic of the inner struggle of the Creator. (See Matthew 27:45.) The anguished Father chose to shield His beloved Son from gawking eyes. An eerie silence settled over the scene, like the ominous hush before a ferocious storm.

On the lightless hill it became hard to see if the Savior was dead or alive. The minutes ticked by slowly in nervous expectation. Periodically an earsplitting lightening bolt caused the ground to shudder, briefly illuminating Jesus' limp and battered form as if from the flashes of a hundred cameras. Many people stumbled away from the forbidding place, gathering up family and wailing about retribution and the end of the world.

At about three o'clock in the afternoon, the general darkness lifted, and the sun once again shone brightly, *yet deep darkness continued to envelope the middle cross*. Fiery shafts of lightning now seemed directed at Christ Himself.[15] A shiver of stark fear rippled through the remaining crowd as heaven's mysterious, supernatural light-and-sound show intensified.

Suddenly, everyone was startled by a loud, terrifying yell, an unnerving scream, that emanated from within the darkness surrounding the center cross and echoed out across Golgotha: " 'My God, my God, why hast thou forsaken me?' "

Time froze as all eyes turned in the direction of that desperate voice. "The fierce temptation that His own Father *had forever left Him*, caused that piercing cry from the cross. . . ."[16] It was the urgent, pleading shout of someone in the grip of hellish circumstances. It was the cry of Someone whose heart was being torn in two by grief. Jesus is described at that moment as "in despair."[17]

Everything Christ now experienced shouted at Him that the separation between Himself and the Father would be eternal. Satan and hundreds of evil angels declared with unnerving certainty that Jesus was now in their hands and no longer in favor with God. They told Him repeatedly that by bearing our sins He was permanently cut off from His heavenly Father and would never be able to see Him again.

The "second death" beast roared in Jesus' ear. He could feel its hot breath on the back of His neck. Its suffocating presence enveloped Him. It was all that He could realize during those long, excruciating hours. Both saved and unsaved die the "first death" at the end of this life. However, after the unsaved are resurrected at the end of time, they then die what is called the "second death," eternal death, forever separated from God. By taking the sinner's place, Christ on Calvary came face to face with the awful prospect of that same kind of forever death. The apostle Paul writes that He "taste[d] [the second] death for every man" (Hebrews 2:9, KJV). And again, "Christ redeemed us from the curse of the law, having become a curse for us" (Galatians 3:13).

Ellen White paints a dreadfully grim picture: "All [was] enshrouded in oppressive gloom."[18] "The separation that sin makes between God and man was fully realized and keenly felt by the innocent, suffering Man of Calvary . . . He had not one ray of light to brighten the future."[19] "The Saviour *could not see through the portals of the tomb.* Hope did not present to Him His coming forth from the grave a conqueror, or tell Him of the Father's acceptance of the sacrifice. He feared that sin was so offensive to God that *Their separation was to be eternal.*"[20]

On Calvary, infinite love suffered infinite hurt. People standing near the cross heard our Lord's groans of misery as He wrestled with the agonizing fear that He could be saying Goodbye to His Father forever. Such torment is beyond our comprehension. We have been given at least one faint glimpse, one slight bridge of understanding, when we read: *"So great was this agony that His physical pain was hardly felt."*[21] Try to imagine the excruciating physical torments of crucifixion, the fiery, teeth-grinding bolts of pain. Now try to imagine a mental and emotional pain so intense that such physical agonies are hardly even felt!

This separation sent shock waves throughout the universe. The sinless beings inhabiting unfallen worlds understood far better than we can what that separation involved, and they were filled with consternation. Note the following thought-provoking insight: "The interruption of the communion between God and His Son caused a condition of things in the heavenly courts which cannot be described by human language."[22]

After languishing in a spiritual abyss, the Savior was bathed in sweat, with hair matted, face ashen, eyes bloodshot and staring, fluid draining from His nose, lips quivering yet wordless. Life was quickly draining away.

In a final, breathtaking leap of faith and trust, Jesus somehow pressed through the thick wall of spiritual darkness and cast Himself upon the mercy of His loving heavenly Father. He knew His Father well and by a stunning act of will chose to place His full confidence in God for the future, no matter what current circumstances seemed to dictate. He placed His full weight on heaven's past acceptance and assurances. "And as in submission He committed Himself to God, the sense of the loss of His Father's favor was withdrawn. By faith, Christ was victor."[23] "Jesus did not die in defeat. He was fully conscious of the triumph that was His and was confident of His own resurrection."[24]

Jesus moved slightly, painfully, against the nails. With all His remaining strength He then drew in a deep, raspy breath, lifted His head, and shouted out the victorious words, " 'It is finished! Father, into Thy hands I commend My spirit' " (John 19:30; see Luke 23:46). A light as bright as the sun encircled the Son, and inner peace at last replaced the terrors of the last several hours. Nonetheless, the ordeal had been too much. His great, loving heart literally burst, and His head slumped forward on His chest in death.

Fast-forward to Sunday morning at the tomb, shortly after the resurrection. We can hardly imagine how anxious Jesus was to ascend to His Father, to feel His loving embrace after all that the Savior had endured. The angelic choir had rehearsed for years for that glorious, supremely triumphant homecoming. The unfallen worlds eagerly awaited their Lord's return. But all of that had to wait because Mary Magdalene was weeping. Jesus told all heaven to wait because she desperately needed to hear His words of assurance and love. He paused, and in His familiar, tender voice, turned to His devoted follower and simply said, "Mary." Drying the tears of one heartbroken person was more important than reuniting with the Trinity or receiving the adoration of millions.

1. Ellen G. White, "The Privilege of Prayer," *Bible Echo*, 1 February 1893, paragraph 7.

2. *The Desire of Ages*, 624.

3. Ibid., 672.

4. Leon Morris, *The Gospel According to Matthew* (Grand Rapids, Mich.: Eerdmans, 1992), 667.

5. *The Desire of Ages*, 686.

6. Ibid., 686.

7. *The Sufferings of Christ*, 15, 16, italics supplied.

8. *The Desire of Ages*, 687, italics supplied.

9. Ibid., 690.

10. Ibid., 689.

11. Ibid., 690.

12. Ibid., 694.

13. See *The Desire of Ages*, 753, 754.

14. Elie Wiesel, *Night* (New York, N.Y.: Bantam Books, 1960), 30, 31.

15. *The Desire of Ages*, 754.

16. *The Sufferings of Christ*, 36, 37, italics supplied.

17. Ibid., 36.

18. Ibid., 38.

19. Ibid., 44, 45.

20. *The Desire of Ages*, 753, italics supplied.

21. Ibid., italics supplied.

22. *Seventh-day Adventist Bible Commentary*, 7A:228.

23. *The Desire of Ages*, 756.

24. *Seventh-day Adventist Bible Commentary*, 5:550.

Chapter 9

Releasing the Dragon

Rob Hall, one of the most respected high-altitude climbers in the world, was in serious trouble. A 35-year-old New Zealander, Hall had hiked up Mt. Everest four times between 1990 and 1995, leading thirty-five climbers to the top. On May 10, 1996, he reached the 29,028-foot summit of Everest again, then suddenly and without warning found himself engulfed by a horrendous blizzard. The weather turned extreme. Whiteout conditions prevailed, and the temperature plummeted dramatically as night approached.

At 4:30 P.M. the radios far below at base camp crackled with an urgent transmission. " 'I need a bottle of [oxygen]!' Hall pleaded in a desperate, breathless voice to anyone on the mountain who might be listening. 'Somebody, please! I'm begging you!' " There was no chance, however, that anyone could reach him under those terrible, life-threatening conditions.

Somehow, Hall survived without shelter during the frigid night of hurricane-force winds and a wind chill of 100 degrees below zero. "During the call at 4:43 A.M., he told Caroline Mackenzie, our Base Camp doctor, that his legs no longer worked, and that he was 'too clumsy to move.' " A short time later Base Camp patched through another call to Jan Arnold, Hall's wife, in Christchurch, New Zealand. " 'My heart really sank when I heard his voice,' " she recalls. " 'He was slurring his words markedly.' "

On May 11, at 6:20 P.M., after being stranded for more than twenty-four nightmarish hours, Hall was patched through again to his wife. " 'I can't tell you how much I'm thinking about you!' he said.

" 'I'm looking forward to making you completely better when you come home,' his wife replied. 'I just know you're going to be rescued. Don't feel that you're alone.' "

"Before signing off, Hall told his wife, 'I love you. Sleep well, my sweetheart. Please don't worry too much.' " These were his last words. Climbers found Hall twelve days later, lying on his right side on the ice, his upper body buried beneath a mound of snow.[1]

Two thousand years ago Jesus Christ was caught in a ferocious spiritual storm. The howling tempest of separation from God swept down upon Him with life-destroying power. Angels in heaven heard His desperate pleas and longed to rescue Him but could not. One of His last transmissions before His death was the words, *"My God, My God, why have you forsaken Me!"*

Of all that Christ said during His thirty-three years of life on earth, these words are, in many ways, the most important. Here is the center of the plan of salvation, the heart of the gospel. If we take the time to try and understand the meaning of those vital, heart-rending words, we can better comprehend what it meant for Him to be cut off from God. *Those words can provide helpful insights not only into the separation on Golgotha but also into the nature of the separation He previously endured in Gethsemane as well.*

Jesus' cry of forsakenness occurred very near the end of His six hours on Calvary and was the fourth of His seven "sayings" as He hung from the nails:

1. " *'Father,* forgive them; for they know not what they do' " (Luke 23:34).
2. " 'Verily I say unto thee, To day shalt thou be with me in paradise' " (Luke 23:43, KJV).
3. " 'Woman, behold thy son! . . . Behold thy mother!' " (John 19:26, 27, KJV).
4. " **'My God, my God, why hast thou forsaken me?' "** (Matthew 27:46).
5. " 'I thirst' " (John 19:28).
6. " 'It is finished' " (John 19:30).
7. " *'Father,* into thy hands I commend my spirit' " (Luke 23:46, KJV).

On the cross, Christ addressed God three times. For His first and seventh sayings He prayed using the name *Father,* a term that reveals a feeling of familiarity and closeness. But in between, after having been engulfed in impenetrable physical and spiritual darkness for three tortuous hours, He sobbed out the words, "My *God*, my *God.*" From about noon until 3:00 P.M. He felt so separated from His Father that He could no longer address Him with intimacy but resorted instead to the much more distant and formal title "God."

Jesus' cry was a direct quote from Psalm 22:1. This stirring psalm predicted several elements of Jesus' suffering. He must have studied and reflected on it many times before. As He experienced the terror of separation from God, His mind naturally and automatically went to that psalm as the perfect expression of what He endured.

Knowing that Christ's words of forsakenness come from Psalm 22:1 enables us to understand their meaning more fully *because of the way the psalm itself was written.* Many of the psalms were composed as Hebrew poetry. It wasn't the kind of poem we think of today that rhymes, like "Roses are red and violets are blue." Instead, the Jews used a type of poetry called "thought parallelism." That simply means that the two halves of a verse are parallel in that they say the same thing but in different words. The thought is repeated.

For example, in the first part of Psalm 22:10 we read, "Upon thee was I cast from my birth." In the second half of that verse the author says the very same thing in another way: "Thou hast been my God from my mother's womb" (Ps. 22:10, NASB).

We can use that insight into Hebrew poetry to help explain Jesus' words from Psalm 22:1. The first half of the verse contains the familiar words:

"My God, my God, why hast thou forsaken me?"

In the second half of that verse, the psalmist repeats the same idea by saying:

"Why art thou so far from helping me, *and from the* words of my roaring [*crying*]?*"*

According to this part of the verse, Christ felt forsaken in two particular ways:

- He received no help.
- There was no audible response to His cries or prayers.

Actually, Jesus' cry of forsakenness on Golgotha connects us to more than just the first verse of Psalm 22. John Luther Mays observes, *"Citing the first words of a text was, in the tradition of the time, a way of identifying an entire passage"*[2] (italics supplied). Therefore, by quoting from the opening verse, Jesus essentially identified Himself with the overall subject matter of the *whole twenty-second psalm.* The twin themes of no help and no response to His cries are prominent in verses 1 through 21 in particular. For example,

> Be not far from me; for trouble is near; for there is *none to help* (Psalm 22:11, KJV).

> O my God, I cry in the daytime, *but thou hearest not;* and in the night season, and am not silent (Psalm 22:2, KJV).

We can now examine those two aspects of His separation from God more fully. We will cover the first in this chapter and the second in the following chapter, "A Terrible Silence."

He received no help

All during His lifetime Christ was "helped" through being carefully guarded by heavenly angels. Having chosen to lay aside His divine powers and inhabit a weakened human body, Christ made Himself extremely vulnerable. Satan and his millions of evil angels could employ their weighty supernatural powers against him. The Lord was also at risk from the hatred of human adversaries. More than once, enraged individuals tried to kill the Savior prematurely. Through it all, heavenly angels provided vital protection.

When I visited the lion exhibit at a zoo recently, I felt very little fear. I'm proud to report that even though I stood only a few feet from several ravenous, man-eating lions, I stood my ground and didn't try to run away or scream. How could I do that, you ask? Huge steel bars, that's how. They were my source of comfort. If I thought for one second that the king of beasts could actually get out and start munching on my scrawny body, I'd never go near that place!

Jesus was comforted by a similar assurance. The devil hated Christ and longed to do Him harm, but the angels acted as steel bars to restrain him. "The Father's presence encircled Christ, and nothing befell Him but that which infinite love permitted for the blessing of the world. *Here was His source of comfort.*"[3]

The "Father's presence" that encircled Christ was a cordon of angelic bodyguards, a kind of heavenly Secret Service. "The angels' work is to keep back the power of Satan."[4] Dwelling in a hostile land, Christ took solace from the knowledge that these heavenly beings were at His side every second of every day.

But, starting at Gethsemane, all that changed. A central aspect of the separation Christ endured was God's removal of angelic help and protection. As the Father pulled back, He withdrew the angel shield, *giving Satan unprecedented access to His Son.*

The devil harmed Christ physically

Once Jesus' angel guard was removed, Satan and his evil angels were allowed, for the first time ever, to harm the Savior physically. In the wilderness the devil had been given permission to carry the Son of God to a pinnacle of the temple and onto an exceedingly high mountain. He could not, however, injure Him. Now, in Gethsemane, the heavenly angels stepped back, and Satan and his wicked cohorts were allowed to arrest Jesus and drag Him through a horrifying series of physical torments.

"[Christ] was to work no miracle for Himself, but angels protected His life *till the time came when He was to be betrayed* by one of His disciples, till He was to give His life on Calvary's cross."[5] "Legions of evil angels were all about the Son of God, yet the holy angels were bidden not to break their ranks and engage in conflict with the taunting, reviling foe. Heavenly angels were not permitted to minister unto the anguished spirit of the Son of God."[6]

Delighted to finally get his hands on Christ, the devil put our Lord through *five trials, four brutal beatings, two flesh-destroying scourgings, and then the horrors of crucifixion.* We can hardly imagine what Jesus must have felt as He was deserted by the One He had depended on since childhood as His best Friend, Shield, and Protector!

The news media once carried the horrifying story of abductors who forcibly highjacked a car from two young parents at gunpoint. The thieves forced them out of the automobile then drove off without realizing that the couple's four-year-old son was still in the back seat. As the hoodlums drove away, they happened to make a "U" turn which took them right past where the parents were standing. As Mom and Dad watched the speeding car go by, they caught a heart-rending glimpse of their precious son looking desperately out the rear window with his hands outstretched. They could see his lips frame the words, "Help me!" And that's much the way Jesus felt on the cross. The word *forsaken* that Christ used literally means "to abandon."[7] He looked heavenward and cried out to God for help saying, "Why have You abandoned Me?"

The Father was actually more than a passive observer. For our sake, He actively chose to hand His Son over to the horrors of mob violence.

As an analogy, imagine a father and his little boy huddled in the living room of their home while a drunken mob clamors outside for the young lad's life. "Throw him out here or else we'll burn the whole place down!" they scream. The boy shivers with fright and clings tightly to his daddy's pant leg. The shouts from outside grow more insistent. The father looks down at his son with tears coursing down his own cheeks and gives him a long, lingering hug. Then he opens the door, places the lad out onto the front step, quickly steps back inside, and locks the door behind him. Through the front window Dad watches in agony as the mob rushes toward his little boy and does things to him that are unimaginable.

Likewise, God the Father allowed the devil to have access to His own Son. The Spirit of Prophecy tells us, "A terrible amazement, as he felt his Father's presence withdrawn from him, had filled [Christ's] divine spirit with a shuddering dread."[8]

As Schilder has commented, Christ "sees the devils rising up against Him, and as He sees it, God is taking the role of the supervisor in the arena, and it is God who releases the lions, the bulls and . . . the dogs against the great martyr . . . God did not do much; but He did everything that needed doing; *He released the dragon*."[9]

The devil did not whip, beat, or crucify Christ personally. He worked through evil angels in human form and through actual human beings as well. "Religious rulers united with Satan and his angels. *They were doing his bidding*."[10]

The devil oppressed Christ mentally and spiritually

After Jesus' angel guard was removed, Satan and his evil angels were allowed to oppress Christ not only physically but also *mentally and spiritually*. This occurred during two distinct time periods—(1) while Jesus prayed in Gethsemane and (2) from around noon to 3:00 P.M. on Calvary. During both of those periods Satan and hundreds of evil angels pressed in next to Christ and were allowed, through their taunts and reviling, to try and crush His spirit. Jesus' hypersensitive nature felt this mental and spiritual oppression far more keenly than physical pain. Several Spirit of Prophecy quotes help us picture this often underemphasized aspect of Jesus' *suffering from the forces of evil*. Ellen White describes Christ's experiences in Gethsemane.

- "Christ was amazed with the horror of darkness which enclosed Him. The temptations of Satan *were almost overpowering*."[11]
- "The suffering Son of God leaves His disciples, for the power of darkness *rushes upon Him with an irresistible force* which bows Him to the earth."[12]
- "The divine light of God was receding from His vision, and He was *passing into the hands of the powers of darkness*."[13]

In the Garden the devil portrayed the situation facing Christ in its "hardest features."[14] Satan tormented the Savior with the crushing thought that His separation from God would be eternal. He repeatedly pressed the dreadful conclusion that if Jesus took our sins upon Himself He would be cut off from His Father forever. The devil also tried to get Jesus to give up by hammering home the point that the very people Christ had invested in the most were acting the worst. "You guided Israel for centuries, and yet they are trying to destroy You. You poured yourself into the disciples for three years, and they'll all forsake You. One is a betrayer, and another will swear he never even knew You." Every fiber of Christ's being abhorred the thought.[15] Satan drove in the punch line, "If this is how the best act, what can you expect from the rest of humankind? Don't you see how absolutely hopeless these sinners are? It is pointless to go on. You are throwing your life away for nothing."

The effect on Christ was murderous. He collapsed onto Gethsemane's chilly ground, overcome with grief and consternation. Life began to bleed out of Him. An angel was sent to temporarily beat back the forces of evil and revive Jesus with words of encouragement.

Later, on Calvary, from about noon to 3:00 P.M., Satan was again given entire access to Christ and mercilessly attacked Him spiritually and mentally a second time. From the increased intensity of Satan's assault, Jesus could tell that the Father had separated Himself fully, completely withdrawing angelic protection. The devil pressed in on the Savior with even greater harshness than in Gethsemane. Ellen White portrays the devil's onslaught at the crucifixion.

- "He [Christ] was *oppressed by the powers of darkness*. He had not one ray of light to brighten the future. And He was struggling with the power of Satan, who was declaring that Christ was in his hands, and that he was superior in strength to the Son of God, that God had disowned His Son, and that he was no longer in the favor of God any more than himself."[16]
- "Satan with his fierce temptations *wrung the heart of Jesus*."[17]

It is important to note that from the arrest in the garden until noon on the cross, the Son of God recovered dramatically from His inner agony and appeared calm, confident, assured, and hopeful regarding the future. *During that period, for the entire time of the trials, the evil angels were allowed to hurt Christ physically but were apparently restrained from oppressing His spirit as they had in Gethsemane.*

This three-phased sequence of events—(1) allowing the devil to oppress

Jesus' spirit in Gethsemane, (2) giving Christ a reprieve from that oppression until noon on the cross, then (3) letting it resume again for the final three hours—could be compared to taking a direct hit by a hurricane. Those vicious East Coast storms are shaped like a doughnut, with home-disintegrating winds racing around a relatively calm center. First there is the initial blast, then the winds die down as the "eye," or center of the storm, passes through, then the back half of the hurricane rages by. That same type of sequence occurred in Satan's mental and spiritual oppression of Christ.

To summarize, then, the first way Christ felt forsaken by God was from the *withdrawal of angelic protection.* The forces of evil were allowed to afflict Him physically, as well as mentally and spiritually. Like the three worthies in the book of Daniel, Christ entered the furnace of affliction where the fires became "exceeding hot" (Daniel 3:22, KJV). Unlike them, however, He felt abandoned and could sense no heavenly representative by His side.

1. Jon Krakauer, *Into Thin Air* (New York: Anchor Books, 1998), 294-308.

2. James Luther Mays, *Psalms* (Louisville, Kentucky: John Knox Press, 1994), 105.

3. Ellen G. White, *Thoughts From the Mount of Blessing* (Nampa, Idaho: Pacific Press, n.d.), 71, italics supplied.

4. *Seventh-day Adventist Bible Commentary* (Hagerstown, Md.: Review and Herald, 1957), 7-A:366.

5. *The Ellen G. White 1888 Materials,* 126.

6. *The Sufferings of Christ,* 45.

7. Leon Morris, *The Gospel According to Matthew* (Grand Rapids, Mich.: Eerdmans's, 1995), 720.

8. Ellen G. White, "The Sufferings of Christ," *The Present Truth,* 18 Feb. 1886.

9. Klaas Schilder, *Christ Crucified* (Grand Rapids, Mich.: Baker Book House, 1940), 404, 405.

10. *The Desire of Ages,* 749.

11. *The Sufferings of Christ,* 15, 16.

12. Ibid., 19.

13. Ibid., 18.

14. *The Desire of Ages,* 687.

15. Ibid.

16. *The Sufferings of Christ,* 44, 45.

17. *The Desire of Ages,* 753.

Chapter 10

A Terrible Silence

The sickening smell of oily smoke, spent gunpowder, and unattended wounds wafted about Lieutenant Colonel John Frost as he crouched in the dank cellar of a heavily damaged school building. At 31, he commanded the 2nd British Airborne Battalion, assigned to capture and hold the Arnhem bridge in Holland during World War II. On September 17, 1944, behind enemy lines, he and his five hundred paratroopers captured the northern end of the vital bridge across the lower Rhine. German SS Grenadiers firmly held the southern end beyond the swirling river. Everyone knew that the bridge could provide the Allies a swift, direct route into the heart of Germany.

On the first day of battle, Frost made the harrowing discovery that all the radios he had been issued were set to the wrong frequency. Unable to communicate with either air support or infantry reinforcements, he eyed the heavy German buildup fifty yards away with dread. British signalmen stuck radio antennas outside and moved the sets constantly but couldn't make contact with anyone.

Over the next three days Frost's battalion was mauled and battered by the enemy until only one hundred fifty men remained. Unable to fully dislodge the British, the infuriated Germans finally brought up huge sixty-ton Tiger tanks to take down every building the 2nd Airborne occupied, brick by brick. "They looked incredibly sinister in the half light," Frost noted. "Like some prehistoric monsters, as their great guns swung from side to side breathing flame."[1]

The earsplitting thunder of German firepower mingled with the crash of concrete and mortar as enemy tanks methodically reduced Frost's hideouts to rubble. After courageously holding out for over sixty nightmarish hours, he knew that the end was near. As enemy forces stormed across the bridge, a British officer knelt next to one of the radios, held the microphone close to his mouth and shouted, "This is First Para Brigade. We cannot hold out much longer. . . . Please hurry. Please hurry."[2] The only response was a brief crackle of static followed by the crushing weight of silence.

In a climactic spiritual battle at a place called Calvary, the Son of God faced the awful effects of a similar yet far more terrible silence. Behind enemy lines, oppressed by evil forces, without any communication from His Father, He cried out on the cross, " 'My God, my God, why hast thou forsaken me?' "

These words are a quote from Psalm 22:1. Two major themes of that psalm indicate that Jesus felt forsaken in at least two ways: (1) He received no help, and (2) there was no response from heaven to His cries. These two difficulties were also part of His separation in Gethsemane.

In the previous chapter, "Releasing the Dragon," we looked at the concept of having "no help." In this chapter we will go further and explore in what sense He felt forsaken by God because of *a lack of communication from heaven.*

No response to His cries

Jesus frequently cried out to God, praying earnestly and effectively. But there were certain times when His prayers took on a special sense of urgency, particularly when He faced certain crises or turning points in His ministry. During those critical junctures His heavenly Father responded very directly and openly to Jesus' prayers, giving Him direct, audible assurance and encouragement that He was on the right track and had Heaven's full approval. The Father gave special words of assurance to Christ on the following four occasions:

- at His baptism,
- in the Wilderness of Temptation,
- on the Mount of Transfiguration,
- and when the Greeks visited Jerusalem during Passion Week.

First assurance. At Jesus' baptism, when He desperately needed assurance that God was with Him as He began His ministry, the voice came from the

Father, " 'This is my beloved Son, in whom I am well pleased' " (Matthew 3:17, KJV). "Here was the *assurance* to the Son of God that His Father accepted the fallen race through their representative."[3]

Notice how important this heavenly communication was to Christ. "The words spoken from heaven at His baptism were *very precious*, evidencing to Him that His Father approved the steps He was taking in the plan of salvation. . . . These tokens, received from His Father, were *inexpressibly precious* to the Son of God through all His severe sufferings, and terrible conflict with the rebel chief."[4]

The devil must have harassed Jesus unmercifully for years with the temptation to think He was deluded. Christ looked like everyone else. He was raised in a normal home. He lived in a common, out-of-the-way village. As far as we know, He did not work any miracles prior to His baptism. And yet He firmly believed He was the Creator of the universe, the great "I Am" of the Old Testament who led Israel out of Egypt, and a full-fledged member of the Holy Trinity.

Surely Satan mocked Christ with the words, "You think you're God Himself? A lowly, dime-a-dozen carpenter, and you think you're all powerful and existed from eternity past? You actually believe such nonsense? You have got to be the craziest person on the planet!" The devil continued, "Talk about visions of grandeur! On what basis are you coming up with these absurd notions?" It is no wonder that the words of approbation from the Father at Jesus' baptism were "inexpressibly precious."

Second assurance. The second assurance takes us into the Wilderness of Temptation. The Father could not speak directly to Christ, because after forty days of fasting and hours of exhausting hand-to-hand spiritual conflict with Satan, the Savior was now faint and dying. Angels revived the Sufferer and then delivered God's message of encouragement. "After the foe had departed, Jesus fell exhausted to the earth, with the pallor of death upon His face. . . . The angels now ministered to the Son of God as He lay like one dying. He was strengthened with food, comforted with the message of His Father's love and the *assurance* that all heaven triumphed in His victory."[5]

Third assurance. Just prior to the Mount of Transfiguration Jesus had shared with His disciples for the first time the shattering news that He would suffer and be killed. He charted a course contrary to the greatest Bible scholars Israel had to offer.

At this critical juncture, "He must Himself gain a fresh hold on Omnipotence, for only thus can He contemplate the future."[6] Jesus pleaded for assurance. The Father responded to Christ's prayer on the mount for confirmation by saying once again, " 'This is my beloved Son, in whom I am well pleased.' " *The same words as at the baptism.* This time the Father also added the admonition to the disciples, " 'Listen to Him.' " Besides giving direct verbal assurance, the Father sent Moses and Elijah to offer encouragement. Luke reveals that they talked about "his departure [death], which he was to accomplish at Jerusalem" (Luke 9:31). "Not the inauguration of Christ as king, but the decease to be accomplished at Jerusalem, is the subject of their conference with Jesus."[7]

Fourth assurance. During Passion Week several Greeks came to Jerusalem to worship and to meet with Christ. In the arrival of these Gentile visitors, He saw an illustration of the impact His sacrifice would ultimately have on the nations of the world. However, as Christ's mind contemplated that upcoming sacrifice, He confessed, " 'Now is my soul troubled' " (John 12:27). The reality of the Cross pressed heavily on His spirit.

Then, once again, the voice came from the Father indicating that He would be glorified by His Son's death—" 'I have glorified [my name], and I will glorify it again [in your death]' " (John 12:28). Jesus said that this time the voice came primarily for others: " 'This voice has come for your sake, not for mine' " (John 12:30). Nonetheless, it is hard to imagine that He Himself didn't find it reassuring and encouraging as well. Ellen White, in fact, tells us that "as the voice was heard, a light darted from the cloud, and encircled Christ, as if the arms of Infinite Power were thrown about Him like a wall of fire."[8] George Knight observes, "Then, in response to His prayer, God's voice came from heaven, *assuring Jesus that He was on the right path.*"[9]

If we charted Jesus' public ministry, we would see these *four major crises*— baptism, wilderness temptations, the Mount of Transfiguration, and the visit of the Greeks—accompanied by *four assurances.*

One morning a friend phoned with the shocking news that a very young mother, whom we both knew, had just been diagnosed with inoperable liver cancer. As her pastor, I stopped by her home that day to visit and offer whatever encouragement I could. At that time she didn't look too ill and seemed to be coping well, buoyed up by her newfound faith in Christ. Relatives and friends were very helpful, and their visits once a week were enough to sustain her courage. As the tumor grew, so did Brenda's desire for emotional support and assurance that God was still in charge. She was eventually hospitalized with a greatly enlarged abdomen and constant, severe pain. Daily visits were now the rule.

The trauma intensified, and her family gladly committed themselves to maintaining a marvelous round-the-clock presence in her hospital room, even though it was many miles away. They held her hand, massaged her back, sang hymns, read Scripture, laughed, cried, reminisced, and prayed at her side on rotating shifts. She responded with a faith and hope that made the doctors marvel.

Many times she invited her three-year-old son to climb up on the bed so she could embrace him tightly with her IV laden arms as long as the pain permitted. Near the end she was taken home, as she had requested, and lay in the sun wrapped in blankets. Frightfully thin, barely able to speak, she repeatedly asked for both her husband and mother, who were at her side constantly, uttering words of assurance and love until she died.

During her great crisis Brenda could count on assurance and encouragement being there when she needed it most. So it was for Christ as He received four assurances at the four most critical points thus far in His ministry.

Fifth assurance. The fifth assurance occurred in Gethsemane. I have set this assurance apart from the previous four because it took place after Jesus experienced, for the first time in His life, the terror of separation from God. In the moonlit recesses of the garden, the Son of God faced a crisis much different, and far worse, than anything He had ever grappled with before. The Savior sensed the Father separating from Him, and throughout the worst of the ordeal in Gethsemane the heavens were silent. God withdrew from Christ, and during the time the Savior sweated blood from battling the forces of evil, there was no word of assurance from His heavenly Father. He experienced the dreadful, life-sapping sense of isolation portrayed in Psalm 22:2: "O my God, I cry in the daytime, *but thou hearest not;* and in the night season, and am not silent" (KJV).

Because of Jesus' terrible sense of aloneness, He felt the need for sympathy "to the very depths of His being" and had a "yearning desire to hear some words of comfort."[10] Full of anguish, the Savior turned to His disciples twice for support. He longed for words of encouragement from His followers, which would bring Him relief and break the influence of the powers of darkness.[11] Tragically, they were asleep.

It was not until after Christ made His decision to go to the cross and collapsed to the ground dying that the angel Gabriel finally came to Jesus' aid. The Savior would have died right there in Gethsemane if assistance had not arrived.[12] God the Father could not speak to Christ audibly because Jesus needed to be revived first. "The angel raises the Son of God from the cold ground, and brings Him messages of love from His Father. He is strengthened and fortified. He has the *assurance* that He is gaining eternal joys for all who will accept redemption."[13] The angel came to help Christ endure so He could die later on the cross. This fifth assurance was reinforced by the dove-like form that descended upon

Christ at the time of His arrest, just as it had after His baptism. It was a reminder that God was with Him now just as He had been back then.

No assurance on Calvary. At the cross, when the crisis of separation from God again engulfed our Lord, when Jesus most needed assurance, the heavens were this time totally closed off and were as brass over His head. Ellen White observes, "At the baptism and at the transfiguration the voice of God had been heard proclaiming Christ as His Son. Again, just before Christ's betrayal, the Father had spoken, witnessing to His divinity. *But now the voice from heaven was silent.*"[14] On Calvary, during those last three hours of forsakenness, there was not only no heavenly voice, *but there was no angel, no dove, no assurance of any kind.*

The Spirit of Prophecy indicates that the complete lack of response from Heaven was a key element in Jesus' sense of abandonment on the cross. "Faith and hope trembled in the expiring agonies of Christ, *because God had removed the assurances* He had heretofore given His beloved Son of His approbation and acceptance."[15]

G. Campbell Morgan writes, "There is no experience of life through which men pass, so terrible as that of silence and of mystery, the hours of isolation and of sorrow, in which there is no voice, no vision, no sympathy, no promise, no hope, no explanation, the hours in which the soul asks why."[16] Such was awful Golgotha. *The words of Psalm 22:1, "Why are you so far from the words of my roaring" (my translation), were certainly fulfilled.*

In summary, on the cross, the removal of physical protection, the oppression by evil angels, plus the absence of communication from heaven all conspired to create within Christ the sense that He was completely forsaken by the One He loved so faithfully. These elements don't fully explain all that He endured during that mysterious, horrific separation and abandonment, but they do help to open our understanding.

The fundamental reason that the Father drew back from Christ at Gethsemane and on the cross was because His Son had voluntarily become our "Sin Bearer." The responsibility, the guilt, for every sin from all over the world since the time of Adam's fall to the Second Coming was laid upon Christ as our Substitute.

Isaiah predicted, "All we like sheep have gone astray; we have turned every one to his own way; and the Lord hath laid on him the iniquity of us all" (Isaiah 53:6, KJV). Peter added, "Who his own self bare our sins in his own body on the tree, that we, being dead to sins, should live unto righteousness: by whose stripes ye were healed" (1 Peter 2:24, KJV). Paul wrote, "For he hath made him to be sin for us, who knew no sin; that we might be made the righteousness of God in him" (2 Corinthians 5:21, KJV).

"The evil works, the evil thoughts, the evil words of every son and daughter of Adam press upon His divine soul. The sins of men called for retribution upon Himself, for He had become man's substitute, and took upon Him the sins of the world."[17]

Christ voluntarily took responsibility for the sins of Cain; Korah, Dathan, and Abiram; all the wicked kings of Israel; Herod, Caiaphas, and Pilate; Hitler, Mussolini, Stalin, Al Capone, Timothy McVeigh (who blew up the Federal building in Oklahoma); and every evil word and deed from all the billions of people who ever lived, including you and me! It is mind-boggling to even imagine! The devil used the fact that Jesus had become our Sin Bearer to mercilessly oppress the Son of God. In Gethsemane and on the cross, Satan recounted the sins of the world to Jesus, portraying them in the most heinous and unredeemable light possible. *And the worse sin appeared, the more perilous Christ felt His own situation appeared, because He had taken those very sins upon Himself.*

"His burden of guilt was so great because of man's transgression of His Father's law, that human nature was inadequate to bear it. . . . The sufferings of martyrs can bear no comparison with the sufferings of Christ. The divine presence was with them in their physical sufferings. There was the hiding of the Father's face from His dear Son."[18]

Jesus suffered the wrath of God toward unrepentant sinners as described by Paul in Romans 1. It has nothing to do with vengeance or anger. The apostle defines a certain aspect of God's wrath by using the phrase "God gave them up" (Romans 1:24, 26, 28). He says that there comes a time when God tearfully removes Himself from sinners and gives them over to Satan because that is the leader they have ultimately chosen. At Gethsemane and at Calvary, that same wrath fell upon Christ with overwhelming force as the Father "gave Him up" to the forces of evil.

For our sake, the Father and Son lived out what will happen to hardened sinners at the final judgment. It is vital to understand that the wrath that fell upon Jesus because He became our Sin Bearer *actually expresses the attitude of the entire Godhead toward sin.* The Father is not the meany here. His judgment on sin reveals the judgment of all the members of the Trinity on the results of evil.

Ellen White describes Jesus' experience on the cross. "The sins of the world were upon Him, and also the sense of His Father's wrath as He suffered the penalty of the law. It was these that crushed His divine soul."[19]

Even though the Father withdrew from Christ, He did not withdraw the Holy

Spirit. "He [Christ] overcame in human nature, relying upon God for power."[20] "The power that inflicted retributive justice upon man's substitute and surety, was the power that sustained and upheld the suffering One under the tremendous weight of wrath that would have fallen upon a sinful world."[21] Jesus felt forsaken but was nonetheless inwardly sustained by the Spirit of God during those terrible hours.

On Calvary, the Savior gathered every ounce of strength and shouted upward in desperation—"My God, my God"—in a final, heroic attempt to bridge the gulf between Himself and His beloved Father. By incredible faith and trust He hung on through the lethal terrors of separation. "Amid the awful darkness, apparently forsaken of God, Christ . . . relied upon the evidence of His Father's acceptance *heretofore given Him.*"[22] He relied especially on the assurances previously received during His ministry.

Finally, God lifted the darkness, and Jesus' face lighted up with a divine glory. His sense of oneness with the Father was restored. But the mental agony and emotional strain had been far beyond the endurance of humanity. His heart literally burst, and the innocent Sufferer was dead. No one forced Him to die. No one imposed that sentence upon Him. No one stole His life from Him. Christ voluntarily chose to lay down His life in this way because of His unquenchable love for our tiny, sin-infected world.

In my imagination I picture the experience of eight-year-old Rueben at Golgotha. For six hours he watched Christ's body convulse against the nails, heard His labored breathing, and wondered at every dry-mouthed word. The young boy's tender heart nearly broke as he witnessed Jesus' terrible plight. This was the Man who enabled his beloved father to come home after two frightful years in a leper colony up north. Rueben's body involuntarily trembled at the Savior's sudden shout, "My God, my God, why have you forsaken me?"

His mind searched for some tangible way of showing Christ that He was not abandoned by everyone, that he still had at least one small friend. Rueben turned, raced down the hill, and stumbled breathless into his family's two-room home in Jerusalem. From under his bed he grabbed the palm branch he had saved from the triumphal entry several days before. He would wave it before Christ once again as a sign of loyalty and devotion.

By the time Rueben arrived back at Calvary, Jesus had already died. Stunned, the young disciple shook his head in disbelief. He held the palm forlornly by his side. Then, suddenly, his heart told him what to do. He tried to maneuver through the crowd but was halted by a Roman spear. "Let the lad go," a tall centurion ordered, pushing the spear aside. "It doesn't make any difference now." Rueben walked forward, knelt down, and tearfully placed the withered, dying palm on the blood-stained ground beneath his Hero on the center cross.

---

1. Cornelius Ryan, *A Bridge Too Far* (New York, N.Y.:Simon and Schuster, 1974), 438.

2. Ibid., 485.

3. *The Sufferings of Christ*, 7, italics supplied.

4. Ellen G. White, *Advent Review and Sabbath Herald*, 18 Aug. 1874; *Seventh-day Adventist Bible Commentary,* 7-A:201.

5. *The Desire of Ages*, 131, italics supplied.

6. Ibid., 420.

7. Ibid., 422.

8. Ibid., 625.

9. George Knight, *My Gripe With God* (Hagerstown, Md.: Review and Herald, 1990), 87, italics supplied.

10. *The Desire of Ages*, 687.

11. Ibid., 690.

12. See Ellen G. White, *Advent Review and Sabbath Herald,* 18 Aug. 1874); *Seventh-day Adventist Bible Commentary,* 7-A:223.

13. *The Sufferings of Christ*, 27, italics supplied.

14. *The Desire of Ages*, 746, italics supplied.

15. *The Sufferings of Christ*, 37, italics supplied.

16. G. Campbell Morgan, *Crisis of the Christ: The Seven Greatest Events of His Life* (Grand Rapids, Mich.: Kregel, 1989), 301.

17. *That I May Know Him*, 66.

18. *The Sufferings of Christ*, 23.

19. Ibid., 44.

20. *Seventh-day Adventist Bible Commentary*, 7-A:228.

21. Ibid., 223.

22. *The Desire of Ages,* 756.

Chapter 11

Lessons: Part A

As we watch Jesus' limp body being taken down from the cross and think back over all that has happened since His arrest, certain lessons stand out. Those lessons, which the sufferings of Christ were designed to teach with unique clarity and force, are essential not only for the inhabitants of this tiny planet but also for the billions of heavenly angels and unfallen beings throughout the universe. Jesus' pain provides a series of vital revelations designed to alter the *thinking* of God's creation in both heaven and earth, and hopefully right thinking would lead to right choices.

It is not my intention in these last two chapters to review the various theories of the atonement that have developed over the centuries. That topic is very important. It has, however, too often generated more heat than light. Sincere Bible students have found themselves hunkered down in their respective foxholes, lobbing religious mortar shells at each other, all in the name of understanding the cross. I will leave that discussion to another time. However, to those familiar with the ongoing debate over the meaning of the Cross, I want to be clear that I believe Jesus' death was substitutionary, atoning, and sacrificial. He died in our stead. He took our guilt upon Himself and paid the price for our sins on Calvary.

My focus here will be limited to some of the vital, lifegiving lessons we can learn from Jesus' sufferings and death. It is my hope that those lessons will have a positive influence on our personal relationship with all members of the Trinity. *The theme of this chapter is the character of God.*

The character of God

I used to avoid studying or writing about the Crucifixion until I felt "holy" enough. If I got mad at my wife or moped around the house in one of my melancholy broods, I refrained from working on divine things until I got "good." I had mentally turned the Cross into a shrine for the best when in fact God specifically designed it as a refuge for the worst.

Imagine a heart-attack victim sheepishly calling 911 and trying to persuade the dispatcher to help: "Look, I know you guys are very busy, and I know I've been eating way too much cholesterol, and I haven't been jogging like I should. I'm really not worthy of having you folks come way out here and help me at all. [Clutches his chest.] I'm sure there are lots of healthy people, with much more self-control, that you'd much rather associate with. I had a heart attack last year, too, and had to call 911 then, and I'm sure you're probably thinking, 'Oh no, not this jerk again!' But I really wish you'd respond. I'm hurting pretty bad [gasping for breath]. I'll try to get myself going as much as possible before you arrive. I promise not to have any more heart attacks this year. No more triple-scoop, double-fudge sundaes either! I really mean it this time. I promise to be good!"

Of course we think that's ridiculous, but why don't we feel it's just as ridiculous to come that way to God? When your clothes get all dirty and smelly, do you say, "Man, I better not take them to the Laundromat, these duds are soooo filthy!" Of course not. When I stink spiritually and run up Calvary's hill, God doesn't frown and say, "Hey, what on earth are you doing here?" Instead He says, "Well, it's about time. What kept you?" It is in fact our desperate sense of need that best qualifies us to come to Calvary. The Cross is the hospital, the Laundromat, and, of course, so much more.

My reluctance to approach God in filthy garments betrayed a fundamental, underlying misunderstanding of who He really is. God is neither repulsed by our need nor impressed with our goodness. He does not have to be persuaded to help us. We do not have to be worthy to approach Him. Only He is good. Only He is worthy. He is always, in every circumstance, eager and anxious for us to come. In fact, the evidence from Jesus' life indicates that God is actually attracted to sinners. The gospel is not primarily good news about how we can get to heaven. It is first and foremost good news about God.

The central message of the cross is the Trinity's love. "For God is love; and his love was disclosed to us in this, that he sent his only Son into the world to bring us life. The love I speak of is not our love for God, but the love he showed to us in sending his Son as the remedy for the defilement of our sins" (1 John 4:9, 10, NEB). "The revelation of God's love to man centers in the cross."[1] Love is not something God chooses. He doesn't wake up in the morning and say, "Well, should I be loving or should I be a real pain? Should I be kind and caring or make people miserable?" He never has to choose whether or not to love. Love is all He knows. Love is all He ever feels like being. Love is not one option among many; it is all there is. It has nothing to do with who we are but everything to do with who He is.

The theology of many individuals grows out of their personality. We create God in our own image. He is either too stern or too milquetoast depending on our own insecurities and hang-ups. Our misconceptions are also fueled by our chronic habit of comparing God's love to what we have experienced in life from others. We think, "God must be like Dad or Uncle Joe or the nice lady at the corner store." That's natural, but flawed. Any love that originates in the human heart, which is produced apart from Christ, is false. It is simply selfishness in disguise. No one can produce the genuine article on his or her own. You can't look at man-made love and then conclude, "Oh, God must be like that." The great news of the gospel is that God is not simply a better version of humanity's own efforts. God is not simply a souped-up version of us. The Good News is that His love is totally different than humanity's counterfeit caring.

Even the love that God pours into us by His Spirit gets terribly warped by our sinful human natures and comes out very far from perfect. You have never personally seen the love of God as it exists within the Godhead. You may have caught faint glimpses from fellow Christians, but that is all. At best you have only seen through a "glass darkly." God's love is so broad, so deep, so wide, so high, so immense, and so wonderfully different that you really have to stretch to even begin to understand it. All your preconceived notions must be shelved.

A neighbor asks, "Hey, Kim, ever seen any big holes in the ground?"

"Oh yeah," I reply. "I was there when they excavated behind my house for our new swimming pool. Man, that was one big hole! I'm talking huge. That baby must have been at least twelve feet straight down. I didn't dare get near the edge. You fall into something like that and you're never coming out. It's probably the biggest hole in the entire world."

Then one day our family visits the Grand Canyon in Arizona, and my hole back home starts looking pretty small. I've ridden a mule down into the bowels of that canyon and also gazed at it through floor-to-ceiling restaurant windows just as the setting sun ignited the upper edges of the great divide. The place is vast! It gave me a whole new perspective. The Cross does that for the love of God.

I am reminded of the story about Flatland. The inhabitants of this imaginary place lived in a two-dimensional world. All they knew were length and width. Their world was utterly flat, like lines on a piece of paper. They had absolutely no concept of "up."

Another group of people lived in a three-dimensional world, where "up" seemed entirely natural and routine. Whereas the citizens of Flatland only knew about flat circles, the people in the three-dimensional world knew all about such amazing things as spheres. Now imagine people from the three-dimensional world trying to explain to Flatlanders what a basketball was like! The Flatlanders might take offense, and the three-dimensional people might get crucified!

The first step toward understanding would be for the Flatlanders to admit that their normal way of looking at things was extremely limited. So it is for us. Our presentations of the love of God can leave people "flat" if we fail to emphasize that God's love is very different from anything they have ever known.

It is an astonishing fact that as Jesus' creation was torturing Him to death and heaping upon Him every abuse and insult imaginable, His love for them actually *grew stronger and stronger*.[2] He loved them more after His sickening ordeal than He did before! It would be an awesome miracle just to have maintained the same level of love, but it actually increased! He loved Annas and Caiaphas more; He loved Herod and Pilate more; He loved the thugs who beat Him, the brutes who scourged Him, the wretches who spat on Him, and the cowards who mocked Him more than before. Their horrifying behavior revealed more fully their need, and Jesus, without any thought for Himself, responded with an increased desire to help. The apostle Paul expressed it this way, "But where sin increased, grace abounded all the more" (Romans 5:20).

Such love should be a deathblow to all attempts to imitate God's character by our own efforts. Can you imagine loving someone more after they have accused your mother of being a harlot and done their best to tear down everything you've labored to build up? Can you conceive of loving people more after they have spread false rumors that caused you to be hunted like an animal and tortured in the most excruciating, humiliating manner possible?

When people tell me that they have committed some big sin or repeated the same one for the hundredth time, they too often go on to say, "And what makes it worse is feeling that Jesus is upset at me!" Oh, what a terrible misconception! The worse we are, the more anxious He is for us to come to Him. God's love only increases in the face of our need, it never decreases. Such a truth is not an encouragement to sin but the greatest possible motivation to quit sinning and return to the One who loves us so.

The apostle Paul wrote, "While we were yet sinners Christ died for us" (Romans 5:8). He taught that while we were still mucking around in self-centered living and running from God, Christ sacrificed Himself for us. That means that His love is not dependent on our goodness. *His love is unconditional.* He doesn't say "I love you if" or even "I love you because." God simply says "I love you, period." His love is like the sun. It shines on us constantly, unfailingly, no matter what.

God's unconditional love provides lasting freedom from insecurity and fear. God says to us, " 'You do not have to be fearful that [my] love will be taken away. You will not be punished for your openness or honesty. There is no admission price to my love, no rental fees or installment payments to be made. There may be days when disagreements and disturbing emotions come between us. There may be times when psychological or spiritual miles lie between us. But I have given you the word of my commitment. I have set my life on a course. I will not go back on my word to you. So feel free to tell me your negative and positive reactions, and your warm and cold feelings. I am committed to your growth and happiness. I will always love you.' "[3]

At the risk of sounding syrupy, it nonetheless must be said that God is passionately in love with you. He says, "I want you to know that I'm committed to you. . . . I'll always in every circumstance seek to help you and support you. If you're down and I can lift you up, I'll do that. Anything I have that you need, . . . I'll give it to you. . . . No matter what happens in the future, either good or bad, my commitment to you will never change. . . . I love you, and that's what it means."[4]

Too many people see God as pictured in the following **incorrect diagram relating to us sometimes out of love, sometimes out of justice:**

INCORRECT!

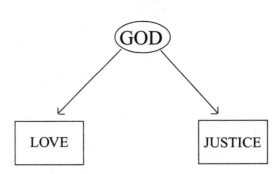

That is a terrible distortion, as if love and justice were somehow separate within the heart of God. Such thinking feeds the heretical idea that God is often loving, but if you get Him riled up, His justice takes over, and He lashes out in anger. Because this thinking divorces justice from love, it perpetuates the devilish perception that God can be harsh and vindictive. God's justice is in fact nothing like ours. Jesus rejected the concepts of revenge and "an eye for an eye" (see Matthew 5: 38, 39).

The truth is that God's love is a unique blend of justice and mercy. Ellen White gave us a tremendously important insight when she wrote, *"God's love has been expressed in His justice no less than in His mercy*. Justice is the foundation of His throne, and *the fruit of His love."*[5] Justice and mercy are wed within the heart of God and are *equally a product of His love*.

The **correct diagram** should be:

CORRECT!

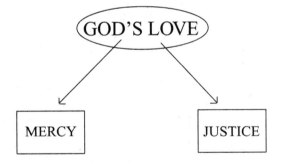

We could even go a step further. We could view the terms *justice* and *mercy* as simply human language trying to describe how God's love expresses itself in different situations. When God forgives a repentant sinner, we call that "mercy." When He judges a hardened sinner, we call that "justice." The truth is that He simply does what His own loving character dictates in every situation. That is the fundamental, root principle out of which He always acts. By way of analogy, water can be manifest as a liquid, steam, snow, or ice, depending on the circumstances. But those are just our labels for what is in every case simply good ol' H_2O. Likewise, justice and mercy are simply different manifestations of the very same fundamental, unwavering love. Even the destruction of the wicked is an act of love, because immortality for them would be misery, and heaven would be torture.

In a sense, God is captive to His own love. His love compels Him to gladly pour Himself out for others. There is this wonderful Being out there in the universe with infinite resources and power, who is intensely in love with you. He will go to extraordinary lengths to win you to Himself. He will bestow on you unimaginable privileges, bend every resource to minister to your joy, and serve your needs, if necessary, to the point of facing self-annihilation. You cannot earn such love, nor can you diminish it. You can choose to accept it, however, and let it change your life forever.

It is this rock bottom, fundamental truth about God's amazing love that must permanently burn its way into our minds. No matter how you interpret other portions of Scripture, this central truth about God cannot change. Drive that stake into the ground and measure all else by it.

The problem of misunderstanding God is particularly acute when it comes to people's warped perceptions of God the Father. He has perhaps suffered most from Satan's terrible distortions.

A wealthy old lady employed me during high school as a part-time gardener. Every once in a while I would catch a fleeting glimpse of her whenever she plucked daffodils or fussed over the roses just outside her ornate front door. Her aged face always remained in shadow, thanks to a gaudy, shoulder-width sunbonnet. I worked around her extravagant home for months but never got to meet her personally. She never said "Hello, young man, I'm glad to have you here." Never even waved to acknowledge my existence. She remained aloof, remote, mysterious.

The most visible eccentricity was her daily drive. Hunched down behind the wheel of a shiny black Mercedes, she pulled up to the end of the long, hedged-in driveway and stopped. Obstinately refusing to look either way, she simply honked the horn exactly five times and then pulled out confidently into whatever traffic might be speeding by.

For years I pictured God the Father that way—remote, stern, unknowable. The devil had done a marvelous job of selling me a pack of lies. The Father has a huge image problem, to put it mildly. Satan has been eminently successful in portraying Him as the Scrooge of heaven. But nothing could be farther from the truth.

"Satan led men to conceive of God as a being whose chief attribute is stern justice—one who is a severe judge, a harsh, exacting creditor. He pictured the Creator as a being who is watching with jealous eye to discern the errors and mistakes of men that He may visit judgments upon them. *It was to remove this dark shadow*, by revealing to the world the infinite love of God, that Jesus came to live among men."[6]

Explaining how loving the Father truly is became the central passion of Jesus' life. He stated plainly, " 'He who has seen me has seen the Father' " (John 14:9). They are mirror images of each other. Whatever Christ said or did came from the Father. Jesus was the conduit through which God could pour His love onto the world. Jesus said, " 'The Father that dwelleth in me, he doeth the works' " (John 14:10, KJV).

If God the Father had been incarnated instead of Christ, we would not have noticed any difference at all. "Had God the Father come to our world and dwelt among us, veiling His glory and humbling Himself, that humanity might look upon Him, the history that we have of the life of Christ would not have been changed in unfolding its record of His own condescending grace. In every act of Jesus, in every lesson of His instruction, we are to see and hear and recognize God. In sight, in hearing, in effect, it is the voice and movements of the Father."[7] You would still hear the words, "Neither do I condemn thee, go and sin no more." You would still see little children asleep on the Father's lap. On the cross we would hear the plea, "Jesus, forgive them, for they know not what they do."

Christ taught that the Father is full of mercy: " 'Be merciful, even as your Father is merciful' " (Luke 6:36). He is incredibly generous: " 'If you then, who are evil, know how to give good gifts to your children, how much more will your Father who is in heaven give good things to those who ask him!' " (Matthew 7:11). He is deeply concerned about our needs: " 'For your heavenly Father knoweth that ye have need of all these things' " (Matthew 6:32, KJV). Jesus taught that the Father's heart so deeply resonates with the suffering here on earth that He is pained over the death of even a little sparrow (see Matthew 10:29). "Not a sigh is breathed, not a pain felt, not a grief pierces the soul, but the throb vibrates to the Father's heart."[8]

Many people identify the Father as the thundering God of the Old Testament and Jesus as the warm, accepting God of the New. That is simply not true. The One who led Israel out of bondage and went before them in all their journeys was none other than Jesus. (See 1 Corinthians 10:4.)

The Cross provides the best, most stunning proof of what is really going on in the Father's heart. John writes, " 'God so loved the world, that he gave his only begotten Son' " (John 3:16, KJV). Any parent can testify that it is much harder to give your own son or daughter to die than to die yourself. When Christ hung on that cross, the Father was not millions of miles away in heaven, sipping lemonade. He came to this earth and stood right next to His Son through the entire dreadful ordeal, without revealing Himself. *In God's heart, He was crucified with Christ.* Which of us could listen to our son scream out, "Dad, why have you forsaken me?" and not come to his aid, for the sake of those who hate you?

Jesus didn't die in order to convince the Father to forgive us. The Father was One of the Ones who thought up the whole idea! The Father doesn't love us because of Christ's sacrifice; He provided the sacrifice because He loves us. The Cross didn't change the Father any more than it changed Jesus. "Through the cross we learn that our heavenly Father loves us with an infinite and everlasting love, and draws us to Him with more than a mother's yearning sympathy for a wayward child."[9]

In one of Jesus' most arresting statements He said, " 'Therefore doth my Father love me, because I lay down my life, that I might take it again' " (John 10:17). In effect Jesus is telling us, " 'My Father has so loved you that He even loves Me more for giving My life to redeem you.' "[10]

The heart of our purpose as a church today is to continue the ministry of Christ by clearing up wrong thinking about God. We are the final part of God's efforts down through the centuries to recover the truth about His love. "The last rays of merciful light, the last message of mercy to be given to the world, is a revelation of His [God's] character of love."[11] Revealing the "glory," or character, of God is at the center of the first angel's message of Revelation 14:6, 7.

I fear, however, that we have too often inadvertently shot ourselves in the theological foot here. So often we have done just the opposite of what God desires! For instance, during one prayer meeting I asked the church members, "What is Jesus doing right now in the heavenly sanctuary?"

They replied, "Oh, He's pleading with God the Father to try and persuade Him to forgive us." That answer is so typical yet so monstrously wrong! Jesus Himself stated plainly, " 'At that day ye shall ask in my name: and I say not unto you, that I will pray the Father for you: *For the Father himself loveth you,* because ye have loved me, and have believed that I came out from God' " (John 16:26, 27, KJV).

The entire sanctuary and judgment scenes in heaven are for the sake of creation. The Father is on our side just as much as Jesus is. The ministry of Christ in the heavenly sanctuary is vitally important, but our description of that ministry should not leave the slightest impression that He is more willing to forgive us than the Father.

I also get very nervous the way many members talk about Calvary. I have asked Adventists, "Why did Jesus have to die?" Too often they reply, "To appease God the Father and take His anger over our sins on Himself." It is almost as if they picture the Father storming around heaven shouting, "These sinners are really getting on my nerves! They're gonna have to pay. I want blood."

That's terrible! Once again we are casting the Father as the meany and Jesus as the rescuer. Don't they remember the Bible verse, "God [the Father] was in Christ, reconciling the world unto himself" (2 Corinthians 5:19, KJV)? His love was made visible through Christ.

We have to be especially careful when we talk about God's wrath falling upon Christ in Gethsemane and on the cross. We may inadvertently find ourselves on the wrong side in the great controversy. *Wrath* does not mean God losing His temper. *Wrath* is the biblical term for the brokenhearted efforts of the whole Trinity to both condemn and eradicate the cancer of sin. Because of the role Christ assumed in the plan of salvation, He endured the wrath of the entire Godhead against evil. The Father could have assumed that role instead. On the cross we see revealed the wrath the Godhead will tearfully bring against sin at the end of time (see Revelation 6:16). The judgment that fell upon Christ is the judgment He Himself will ultimately have to exercise against evil. The members of the Godhead have different roles in the plan of salvation, but They love us the same. They forgive us the same.

Within Adventism there is a lingering, fundamental misunderstanding about the Father among the very people who were raised up to clear those distortions away! Instead of scattering the darkness, careless presentations of the sanctuary, judgment, and Calvary only deepen it! The fire department is out starting fires. As a result, for too many Adventists, the Good News about the Godhead is really only Good News about Christ and the Spirit. The Father remains a shadowy figure who dilutes our assurance of salvation and makes us jittery about the judgment. Jesus came to teach us that the Trinity is entirely Good News.

The following quote from the Spirit of Prophecy should give us pause: "In the popular churches, we hear but little except, 'Do you love Jesus?' The love of the Father is scarcely mentioned; it is only Christ, Christ. God the Father has given unto man the greatest gift that Heaven held."[12]

Ellen White beautifully expands our mental picture of the Father when she writes, "All the paternal love which has come down from generation to generation through the channel of human hearts, all the springs of tenderness which have opened in the souls of men, are but as a tiny rill to the boundless ocean when compared with the infinite, exhaustless love of God. Tongue cannot utter it; pen cannot portray it. You may meditate upon it every day of your life; you may search the Scriptures diligently in order to understand it; you may summon every power and capability that God has given you, in the endeavor to comprehend the love and compassion of the heavenly Father; and yet there is an infinity beyond. . . . Eternity itself can never fully reveal it."[13]

To the central questions in the great controversy, "Is God truly loving" and "Can God be trusted?" Calvary answers a resounding "Yes!"

1. Ellen G. White, *God's Amazing Grace* (Hagerstown, Md.: Review and Herald, 1973), 178.

2. *Testimonies for the Church,* 2:212.

3. John Powell, *The Secret of Staying in Love* (Niles, Ill.: Argus, n.d.), 68.

4. Jerry Cook, *Love, Acceptance and Forgiveness* (Ventura, Calif.: Regal Books, 1979), 13.

5. *The Desire of Ages,* 762.

6. Ellen G. White, *Mind, Character, and Personality* (Nashville, Tenn.: Southern Publishing Association, 1977), 1:250.

7. Ellen G. White, *Manuscript Releases,* vol. 21, The Melbourne Camp Meeting, 393.

8. Ellen G. White, *Colporteur Ministry* (Nampa, Idaho: Pacific Press®, 1953), 116.

9. *Seventh-day Adventist Bible Commentary* (Hagerstown, Md.: Review and Herald, 1957), 253.

10. *Steps to Christ,* 14.

11. Ellen G. White, *Christ's Object Lessons* (Hagerstown, Md.: Review and Herald, 1941), 415.

12. Ellen G. White, *Advent Review and Sabbath Herald,* 4 May 1876.

13. *Mind, Character, and Personality,* 1:251.

Chapter 12

Lessons: Part B

Christ knelt down, gathered a mound of sand and clay, then molded and sculpted it. His fingers shaped Adam's fingers, as well as the rest of his body, from head to toe. Jesus spent the most time on the handsome facial features, crafting a regal-looking forehead, a bold chin, and captivating eyes. Then He stood back and gazed at this brand new being and grinned. In many ways Adam was so much like Himself. Christ could hardly wait to give him life so that they could establish a relationship of unparalleled intimacy.

Christ bent down again and placed His mouth onto the inanimate lips of the clay figure. He drew in a deep breath and slowly let it out. Suddenly healthy flesh appeared. The toes wiggled. The hands moved. The eyes opened and stared into the face of Christ. Adam smiled. Together they rose and hugged in a long, lingering embrace.

Expectantly Jesus soon fashioned another wonderful being, incorporating into her form a rib from man as a sign of closeness. Fully equal to Adam, Eve was molded with the very same care and exquisite attention to detail.

Unlike the animals, who were created by the word of God alone, man and woman were fashioned by Christ through personal touch and close personal associations. The way human beings were first created illustrates the extraordinary degree of intimacy God longs to have with each of us today.

Ever since Adam and Eve rebelled, the Godhead has been trying to recover the extraordinary oneness that was demolished in Eden. The Trinity's recovery effort reached its high point in the earthly life of Jesus. Ellen White identifies three milestones during Christ's ministry that were of particular significance in re-establishing our lost intimacy with God—the Wilderness Temptations, Gethsemane, and the Cross. There are a number of parallels between all three experiences that have rarely been explored. Seldom do we hear, for instance, much said about the fact that Jesus became a "Sin Bearer" during those forty days in the desert.[1] The connections between the wilderness sufferings at the beginning of Jesus' ministry and His sufferings during Passover week deserve far greater study.

As we focus here on gleaning lessons from the final events in Jesus' life, we must always keep in mind the big picture—the intense longing of the Godhead to draw us close to Themselves in love. The theological word to describe that grand theme is the *atonement,* or at-one-ment. "God's love for us is not a cold theory or a textbook formula. It is a living, passionate, searching love. Christianity is a love story. The Bible is a divine love letter from One who is forever reaching out to his people."[2] The initiative for accomplishing that oneness is all with God.

In order to develop a deep relationship with the Trinity, it is critical that we understand the lessons They intended for us to learn from the sufferings of Christ. In the previous chapter we reflected on the character of God. *In this final chapter we will explore several more lessons from the sacrifice of the Son of God.*

The source of our worth

Little three-year-old Rebecca stood with her parents at a nearby park to see her very first Fourth of July fireworks display. Thousands gathered at night to see the multicolored lights burst overhead. This also happened to be Rebecca's birthday. As the festivities began, she looked around in delight and then said to her mother, "All this for my birthday?" Her mind wrestled with the thought that all this effort, all this expense, could actually be for her. Likewise, we can look at the plan of salvation, at all the sacrifice by the Trinity, and have a hard time coming to grips with the thought, "All this for me?" Unlike the fireworks, this really is for you.

God doesn't attach such enormous worth to us because of our good looks, our high IQ, or our volunteer efforts at the local soup kitchen. *He gives us infinite value purely as a gift.* God says, "I choose to elevate you to unimaginable importance in My eyes. It is My choice alone, based on what is in My own heart, not yours." We cannot earn such worth by our goodness or lose it by our bad-ness. He bestows it on us out of love.

It is amazing that God values us so much when we consider that our world is only a microscopic speck in the universe. Imagine the size of the universe being drastically reduced so that the sun became the size of the period at the end of this sentence. At that scale, how big would our entire Milky Way Galaxy be? The size of a city block? No. Five miles wide? No. At that scale, our own galaxy would still be a mind-boggling 600,000 miles across![3] I can imagine the unfallen beings poring over their computer star charts for days trying to locate earth in the vastness of interstellar space.

It is also amazing that Jesus valued us so much that He was willing to take an incredible personal risk to save us. Christ triumphed marvelously, but as He walked this earth, there were never any guarantees. "He took the nature of man, with the possibility of yielding to temptation."[4] *By coming here on a rescue mission, He took a personal risk that is absolutely shocking.* Even Heaven itself was put at risk for our sake. Who can calculate the full meaning of the following quotes from the Spirit of Prophecy?

- "[God] permitted Him to meet life's peril in common with every human soul, to fight the battle as every child of humanity must fight it, *at the risk of failure and eternal loss.*"[5]
- "Could Satan in the least particular have tempted Christ to sin, he would have bruised the Saviour's head [ref. Gen 3:15]. . . . Had the head of Christ been touched, the hope of the human race would have perished. *Divine wrath would have come upon Christ as it came upon Adam.* Christ and the church would have been without hope."[6]
- "Remember that Christ risked all. . . . He staked even *his own eternal existence* upon the issue of the conflict. *Heaven itself was imperiled for our redemption.*"[7]

Even with so much at stake, He refused to employ His godly powers on His own behalf. When Jesus walked this earth, people almost universally discounted His divinity. Today we are in danger of discounting his humanity. We can make the awful mistake of thinking He entered the earthly arena able to use His divine attributes to help Himself. The truth is that He faced hardship and temptation the same as we do. The rules of battle dictated that He overcome using no other power than is available to us. Many say "Well, of course Christ conquered—He was God!" But He laid all that aside. *He Himself did not benefit in the least from*

His own divinity. Instead of drawing strength from within Himself, Jesus spent night after night in prayer receiving strength from His Father.

Far from being an asset, Jesus' divinity was for Him, in many ways, a terrible personal liability. Suppose you were hanging unjustly on a cross with huge rusty nails ripping into your flesh. A hostile mob shouts up at you, in words dripping with sarcasm, "Hey, if you're really who you say you are, come down from that cross, you fool!" How much of a temptation is that for you? None, because you know you couldn't get off that cross for a million bucks. But Jesus could! He could have destroyed all His tormentors by a single thought—laid them all out like cordwood.

And if Jesus had utilized His divinity on His own behalf just once, He would have failed to be our example of how to live by faith. "Christ was put to the closest test, requiring the strength of all His faculties to resist the inclination, when in danger, to use His power to deliver Himself from peril and triumph over the power of the prince of darkness."[8] Throughout His ministry, Christ wrestled time and time again with the terrible temptation to use His unlimited divine power for His own benefit.

We cannot imagine the pressure Christ lived under every day! He became the object of every weapon of hell. If He gave in and sinned just once, by thought, by impatient look, or by harsh tone of voice, the entire universe would have been thrown into chaos, and billions of beings would have been lost. He had to be perfectly loving every second, every hour of every day, for thirty-three long, extremely difficult years. If He did sin, He could not simply ask for forgiveness and go on. *There was no second chance.* How easy it would have been to become despondent, depressed, angry, anxiety ridden, or to go just plain crazy! No other human being has ever faced a trillionth of the shuddering responsibility He shouldered every day. If we had to take on those burdens for just one minute, we would be crushed. And He felt that we were worth all the hardship, all the incredible risk!

All this extraordinary effort and risk-taking on the part of the Godhead shouts at us that lost people are extremely important to God. He will not rest until every possible wandering sheep, lost coin, and prodigal son is found and safe. If the lost matter so much to God, they should matter deeply to us as well.

Satan unveiled

Suppose you read the newspaper headline "Abe Lincoln Accused of Being a Traitor!" or "Mother Theresa Accused of Being a Diabolical Liar and Anarchist!" Wouldn't you immediately dismiss those reports as absurd hoaxes? That is similar to the situation the unfallen angels faced in heaven when they first heard the news that Lucifer had turned bad. "No way," they said. "I can't conceive of such a thing." He had been the golden boy of the universe—admired, looked up to as a role model for everyone.

Jesus commented during His public ministry, " 'He [the devil] was a murderer *from the beginning,* and has nothing to do with the truth, because there is no truth in him' " (John 8:44). At the very outset of Satan's rebellion, Jesus saw what no one else could, that sin had turned Lucifer into a destroyer at heart. Because of the Cross, that truth was now manifest for all to see. The devil could destroy sinners and claim they deserved it. But to murder the most loving, innocent Person who ever lived left him without excuse. Jesus said in reference to the Cross, " 'Now shall the ruler of this world be cast out' " (John 12:31). The devil's friendly voice is the voice of a killer.

We only know Satan as Satan. If we had known him before his rebellion and could see the terrible transformation sin has caused, we would be far more appalled at the degrading power of evil. In Satan's life we see that sin, left unchecked, will ultimately seek to destroy every rival to its supremacy, even God.

The truth about human nature

At times I have heard preachers attempt to move their hearers to contrition by pointing an accusing finger at them and declaring, "We all killed the Son of God!" But how could that be, since I wasn't anywhere near the cross? Well, first of all, my sins were part of the load of guilt that broke His heart. Secondly, the same human nature that was in the men who thirsted for His death is inside me. In watching them, I see an illustration of what I could do apart from the grace of God. "The terrible scenes of the crucifixion revealed what humanity will do when under Satan's control."[9]

A church administrator was driving along a busy street when suddenly a pedestrian stepped right out in front of his car. Screeching to a stop one inch from the man's kneecap, the driver, a dedicated Christian, thought, *I'd like to kill that guy!* Startled by such a vengeful thought, this church leader could hardly believe he was capable of such a reaction. The truth is that we are all capable of such dark thoughts, and worse, and might as well admit it. Only the Holy Spirit and the fear of punishment keep us from carrying them out.

As sinners we have lurking within us an innate resentment of authority. Sin strengthens the part of us that detests the authority of God.[10] Culture and education paint it over, but it is nonetheless there. Even babies are self-absorbed and want their own way, now. "Me first!" is the battle cry of every infant. When their needs aren't met, they scream. As adults we have far more sophisticated methods of getting our own way by making others feel anxious, guilty, or stupid if they don't adopt our plans or ideas.

I think it would be a lot more interesting and straightforward if we adults simply cut out the sly stuff and just used the same method that worked so well for us as babes. My boss doesn't give me a raise, so I pound on my desk, stomp my feet, and bawl at five hundred decibels for a couple of hours. The bank turns down my car loan, so I just sit there in the manager's office and scream at the top of my lungs. You know that deep down we still feel like doing that but don't in order to avoid being embarrassed or sent off to an institution.

Apart from the Holy Spirit's work, we are incapable of acting out of purely selfless motives. Apart from a spiritual heart transplant from God, self-interest and sin mar everything we do. We cannot produce any righteousness on our own. None. (See Romans 3:10.) Paul gave us the key to new life: "I have been crucified with Christ; it is no longer I who live, but Christ who lives in me" (Galatians 2:20).

The separation that sin causes

Jesus' words " 'Why hast thou forsaken me?' " reveal that, at its root, sin separates (see Isaiah 59:2). It poisons and destroys relationships. It is a mindset, a built-in attitude that says, "I want to run my own life without interference from anyone else, especially God." At the judgment, those for whom this attitude has become a way of life will receive their wish. God will very reluctantly separate Himself from them, forever.

It was separation from God that killed Christ. *Jesus died* on *the cross, not* from *the cross.* The cross was one of the tortures He endured, along with the beatings and scourgings, but the nails had little if anything to do with His death.

On the cross, Gethsemane happened all over again. *The cross was Gethsemane number 2*, but with greater severity and without any angelic intervention. That was what broke His heart and killed Him—abandonment by God and the crushing weight of the sins of the world. The first separation happened on a hill called the Mount of Olives and the second on a hill called Calvary.

Two hills, two Gethsemanes. They were essentially the same kind of experience. Both were lethal. When talking about the death of Christ, we must look past the nails, past the cross itself. He died from experiencing the second death of forsakenness from God. Christian martyrs only faced the first death; He faced the second.

"Beholding Jesus upon the cross of Calvary arouses the conscience to the heinous character of sin as nothing else can do."[11] Sin is as infectious and devastating as the dreaded Ebola virus. Ebola produces a gruesome death. The skin becomes covered with red blotches. Heart muscle softens, and all the vital organs quickly turn to oatmeal mush. Cramps and convulsions rack the body. Blood pours out of every orifice. Even the eyes bleed. Ebola is one of the most aggressive, lethal viruses on the planet.

Sin has a similarly devastating affect on the soul. God is like the head of a spiritual "Centers for Disease Control," faced with a lethal Ebola-like epidemic of sin covering our entire planet. We see Him in Scripture trying to make the best of a very bad situation. He takes sin extremely seriously because He cares so deeply and knows how harmful it can be. God hates sin like a mother hates the cocaine and heroine that are destroying her son. God's love must take drastic action in order to save as many of us as possible. The Flood, for instance, was God having to cut off a gangrenous limb to save the body. God's love cannot be passive in the face of evil.

"In God's eyes sin is not a trifling matter that He can lightly dismiss, letting bygones be bygones. Sin destroys lives, and its insidious nature threatens cosmic trust in God. God chose not to sit idly by while sin destroyed His creation. He has condemned sin to death wherever it is found."[12]

God's "wrath" is the part of His love that condemns evil and does what is necessary to eradicate it. At the end, the Trinity will have to actively choose to rid the universe of sin. Heartbroken, God will ultimately have no other choice but to destroy sin and sinners. "By a life of rebellion, Satan and all who unite with him place themselves so out of harmony with God that His very presence is to them a consuming fire. The glory of Him who is love will destroy them."[13]

Thank God that, like the Israelites who were bitten by poisonous snakes in the wilderness, we can look to the cross and live!

Belonging to the family of God

Lepers stank. Their flesh looked grotesque, their clothes were ragged and stained, their sores oozed pus, and their breath was foul. Gaunt and haggard, they withered under the debilitating effects of gut-wrenching loneliness. Every sunrise meant another long day of fear and self-loathing. Despair seeped into their bones, and suicide appeared more and more attractive.

Then came Jesus. Everyone else looked at lepers and said "Yuck!" then ran away, but He looked at them and said "I love you" and drew near. Christ's eyes filled with tears whenever He heard a leper utter that awful cry, "Don't come near me. I am unclean." He knelt beside them and touched the putrefying flesh to convey acceptance and bring healing to the heart. Then He spoke the words that made their bodies well.

When the lepers saw Jesus approach, they could have thrown a blanket over their wounds to look more presentable. But none of that mattered. All they needed to do was come, to admit their need and desire to be made whole. So it is with us today. The apostle John wrote with confidence, "If we confess our sins, he is faithful and just to forgive us our sins, and to cleanse us from all unrighteousness" (1 John 1:9, KJV).

Can we imagine that after Jesus endured so much suffering He is pleased to hear us say, "I don't know if I am saved or not. I hope so." How would I feel if my daughter told people she hoped she belonged to our family?

The apostle Paul wanted his readers to be sure they belonged when he wrote, "But now in Christ Jesus you who once were far off have been brought near in the blood of Christ. . . . So then you are no longer strangers . . . but . . . members of the household of God" (Ephesians 2:13, 19).

Ellen White wrote, "You have confessed your sins, and in heart put them away. You have resolved to give yourself to God. Now go to Him, and ask that He will wash away your sins and give you a new heart. Then believe that He does this *because He has promised.* . . . Through this simple act of believing God . . . you are as a child born into the family of God, and He loves you as He loves His Son."[14] We stand before Him in His righteousness, as if we had never sinned.

The beloved John taught, "I write this to you . . . that you may know that you have eternal life" (1 John 5:13). It is not humble to be uncertain about our eternal destiny. We should reject on-off religion where we are saved one minute then commit a sin and are lost the next. Once we have made the fundamental switch from rebelling to submitting, we have salvation. As long as we invite Jesus to be our best Friend and Lord of our lives, we can be assured of salvation by the grace of God. *That assurance remains as long as that fundamental, basic life orientation remains.* Assurance is ours unless we choose to completely turn our backs on God, either by a conscious decision or neglect.

After conversion we obviously need to ask God for victory over sin, but when we trip up and fall, it does not instantly cancel our salvation, any more than an argument between a husband and wife means they are divorced! As long as that couple's fundamental commitment is intact, then the marriage is intact. Likewise, we may often fall flat on our spiritual faces, but that doesn't mean we are divorced from God. As one man put it, "I may have dropped the soap, but that doesn't mean I've stepped out of the shower."

Eternal life is not cheap—it cost the death of God's Son. But it is a 100-percent free gift to those who acknowledge their need and choose it. As soon as you ask Christ to be your Savior, He treats you as a full-fledged son or daughter and pours enormous resources into your life to hold you close to Himself and enable you to grow.

The importance of the law
Satan has tried to have a field day telling lies about the law of God. He specializes in promoting the idea that the law has been discarded as obsolete, harsh, and impossible to keep.

In Christ, heaven has provided two irrefutable answers.

The first answer is how Jesus lived. The Savior affirmed and upheld the law by living it out every day, by reconnecting it with Love. He refused to deviate from the law, even to the point of death. Calvary was, in fact, the ultimate expression of obedience and commitment to the servanthood principles of the law. Christ "became obedient unto death, even death on a cross" (Philippians 2:8). He lived the law perfectly for our sake, in order that His righteous life might be ours. He totally refuted the devil's charge that the law could not be kept.

The second answer is how Jesus died. Jesus' second-death experience proved that the law is very much alive and well. To give an admittedly imperfect illustration, suppose a bunch of my friends and I are running around on top of the Empire State Building saying, "The law of gravity is a lie. The law of gravity is nothing but a great big mindless hoax." Then someone from a security agency comes over and points us to a poster on the wall. At the top, in large letters, are the words, "Don't Let This Happen to You!" Underneath is a grisly photograph of someone who jumped splattered on the street below us. Very ugly scene. I look at my friends and say, "Uh-oh. Looks like we were wrong."

Heaven is banking on sinners having that same kind of "Uh-oh" reaction when it comes to the law of God. What Christ endured proved that the law must still be very much in effect. We see the consequences for Jesus when He suffered, in our stead, the full results of law breaking—separation from God. At the cross the truth was forcefully presented regarding the unchanging nature of the Ten Commandments and the law of Love they embody.

And if the law and its penalty could not be altered to spare God's only Son, how can we imagine that they can be altered to spare spiritual rebels in the judgment? The Cross reveals that God's loving justice is real and will ultimately be compelled to eradicate sin. Calvary draws the curtain back on the future and reveals to the entire universe the final end of those who continue to live as if

God's law doesn't matter. That's why you and I so desperately need a Savior.

God's law is not arbitrary like a 45-mph speed limit or an IRS regulation. His law is simply a description of who He is. It describes the moral core of the entire universe, the way things are inherently designed to run. I can put sand in my car's gas tank—I have that freedom—but that doesn't alter the fact that my auto will be ruined. Someone could protest, "It's a stupid rule that engines can't run on sand." But that doesn't alter reality. The universe was designed to run on love and dependence on God. Anything less is a recipe for disaster.

Obviously, valuing God's law does not enable us to keep it in our own strength. Understanding the debilitating effects of sin does not give us the power to overcome. We are just as dependent on Jesus to live His life as we are to receive His forgiveness. It is vital to realize that Christ died not only to deliver us from the penalty of sin but also from its power. He longs for us to be not only pardoned but also restored. The Cross was designed to make us whole. *"It is the heaven-ordained means* by which the righteousness of Christ may be not only upon us, but in our hearts and characters."[15]

We are saved by grace received through faith, and we become like Christ in the very same way. Everything we need in the Christian life, from repentance to love, is a 100-percent gift. Only God can keep His law within us through His Holy Spirit. "For it is God which worketh in you both to will and to do of his good pleasure" (Philippians 2:13, KJV). "It is the grace of Christ alone, through faith, that can make us holy."[16] Even that new life is so imperfect that Christ's righteousness must cover us continually.

Strength in weakness

Christ had to overcome evil on a daily basis in a mind and body weakened by four thousand years of humanity's sin. *At times, however, he was disadvantaged far beyond that.* On three occasions the devil was allowed to attack the Son of God with amazingly intense temptations and trials—in the wilderness, at Gethsemane, and on the cross. At each of those climactic encounters, when Satan was at his strongest, Christ was at His very weakest. In order to provide spine-tingling proof of the Holy Spirit's power, God the Father asked Jesus to enter each of those momentous spiritual contests in an astonishingly debilitated state.

In the wilderness, Christ met Satan's grueling temptations only after eating nothing for forty long, hot, life-sapping days. By the time the devil came at Jesus with his most difficult temptations, the Son of God was already starving, haggard, and emaciated. He is described as in "extreme suffering."[17] Christ was so weak that after the three temptations were over He fell dying to the ground.

Three years later, when the devil was allowed to attack Christ spiritually in Gethsemane, the Son of God was dying from the emotional trauma of separation from His Father.

Then God the Father, in effect, said to Jesus, "I'm going to permit the devil to attack you on a hill called Calvary with the most powerful, the most horrible, temptations anyone has ever faced. But before that happens, I'm going to allow You, My Son, to be beaten four times, scourged twice, and repeatedly placed on trial. You will hurt so badly that when You fall the second time while trying to carry Your cross, the Roman soldiers will pronounce You dead. Then I'm going to allow them to nail You to a terrible cross, and I'll separate Myself from You once again, as I did in Gethsemane. Finally, when You are in the lowest possible state spiritually, mentally, and physically, full of pain and suffering, hanging between heaven and earth, I'll let the devil come at You on Golgotha with the most terrible temptations he can devise."

When we put the whole picture together—all that was at stake; Christ voluntarily becoming utterly depleted and vulnerable; plus the enormous strength of the devil's temptations—these three occasions become historic instances of unparalleled, lionhearted courage. By His willingness to take on those three wrenching assignments—the wilderness, Gethsemane, and the Cross—while in such a terribly weakened state, Christ revealed Himself to be, without question, the bravest Man who ever lived! He exhibited stunning faith and dependence on God. These episodes in Jesus' life give new meaning to Paul's statement, "When I am weak, then I am strong" (2 Corinthians 12:10).

Because of Christ's experience, there need no longer be any doubt that no matter how weak or undone we may feel there is power enough available in God.

God's incredible solution

Physicists for centuries had wrestled with the seemingly impossible task of understanding the relationship between energy and matter. Generations of scientists examined the problem and came away scratching their balding heads. Even the best efforts involved impossibly convoluted equations that lead nowhere. Then, after lengthy research, Albert Einstein walked up to the blackboard, scribbled out the letters $E=mc^2$, and the problem was solved. A straightforward solution, remarkable in both its simplicity and elegance.

Long ago, when the Trinity put together the plan of salvation, They faced an infinitely more difficult and complex problem—*how to forgive sinners without creating all kinds of potentially disastrous misunderstandings*. The watching universe could have inquired, "How can you simply forgive those rebels like that and wipe the slate clean as if nothing at all had happened?" And Satan would certainly have a field day sowing seeds of doubt and mistrust in God. By forgiving sinners, the Godhead could be charged with being soft on sin, devaluing the law, setting aside justice, and misusing mercy, to name a few.

In Their hearts the Trinity longed to forgive, but They had to deal with these issues first. They had to remove these barriers to forgiveness. The members of the Godhead also had to be true to the mercy and justice within Themselves. The problem had cosmic implications and seemed intractable. How could all these potentially disastrous threads of misunderstanding be resolved in order to extend forgiveness to sinners without creating chaos?

Calvary was the solution. At its core, the answer was one Man, on one cross, for six hours, and all was solved! It was an answer that stunned the universe in its simplicity and depth of sacrifice. The Cross dealt with every significant misunderstanding and nailed down the truth for the whole universe to see. Jesus' substitutionary death on the cross was an absolute necessity because it affirmed both the justice and mercy of God, upheld the integrity of the law, exhausted the law's penalty, judged sin, and guaranteed the eternal stability of God's government. The Cross revealed the truth about the central issues in the great controversy. Without the Cross the barriers would have remained. That is why "without the shedding of blood [on the cross] there is no forgiveness of sins" (Hebrews 9:22).

Edward Heppenstall provides this helpful perspective: "There is a necessity in the divine nature that when sin is forgiven it must be forgiven *in such a way* as to make unmistakable the total opposition of God to sin. . . . At the cross, all members of the Godhead manifested their judgment on sin. Christ became a man in order to assume that judgment and confess it before the universe on behalf of all members of the Trinity. His sacrifice is that of the entire Godhead."[18]

The apostle Paul taught that God gave His Son to die "to demonstrate his justice now in the present, showing that he is himself just and also justifies any man who puts his faith in Jesus" (Romans 3:26, NEB). Because of the Cross, God could now forgive, or justify, the sinner without creating the impression that the justice within His own character was being nullified.

George Knight adds, "Christ's death put God's forgiveness on a moral foundation. Because of the propitiatory sacrifice that demonstrated His consistency and justice, God is free to forgive and justify sinners who accept Christ and still be just Himself. God's love is a moral love."[19]

The apostle Paul exclaimed that through Christ's sacrifice God was able to "reconcile to himself all things, whether on earth or in heaven, making peace by the blood of his cross" (Colossians 1:20). The dilemma posed by sin has been solved; the hindrances to forgiveness have been reconciled. Ellen White observes, *"Every barrier was then broken down* which intercepted the freest fulness of the exercise of grace, mercy, peace and love to the most guilty of Adam's race."[20] "By dying in our behalf . . . [Christ] removed from God all charge of lessening the guilt of sin. . . . He says, . . . By My death a *restraint is removed* from [God's] love. His grace can act with unbounded efficiency."[21]

The tearing down of the barriers to forgiveness came completely at the initiative of the Godhead, while we were yet sinners, still spitting in God's face. At infinite expense the Trinity provided what was necessary to enable Them to save us. It cost Them immense personal suffering. It cost the Godhead everything They had. Praise be to God for His wonderful Gift! "To the only wise God our Saviour, be glory and majesty, dominion and power, both now and ever. Amen" (Jude 25, KJV).

---

1. *Confrontation,* 36, 38.
2. James Bryan Smith, *Embracing the Love of God* (New York: HarperSanFrancisco, 1995), 16.
3. Herbert Friedman, *The Amazing Universe* (Washington, D.C.: National Geographic, 1975), 32.
4. *The Desire of Ages*, 117.
5. Ibid., 49, italics supplied.
6. *Seventh-day Adventist Bible Commentary,* 5:1131.
7. Ellen G. White, *The General Conference Bulletin,* 1 Dec. 1895.
8. *Confrontation*, 85.
9. Ellen G. White, *Signs of the Times,* 12 July 1899.
10. *Steps to Christ,* 34.
11. Ellen G. White, *Maranatha* (Hagerstown, Md.: Review and Herald, 1976), 99.
12. George Knight, *My Gripe With God*, 65.
13. *The Desire of Ages*, 764.
14. *Steps to Christ*, 49, 50, 51.
15. *Seventh-day Adventist Bible Commentary*, 7-A:668.
16. *Steps to Christ*, 60.
17. *Confrontation*, 41.
18. *The Sanctuary and the Atonement* (Hagerstown, Md.: Review and Herald, 1981), 672, 687.
19. *My Gripe With God*, 67.
20. *Seventh-day Adventist Bible Commentary*, 7-A:669, italics supplied.
21. *That I May Know Him*, 69, italics supplied.

THE GIFT

Discussion Questions

Chapter 1   <u>The Traveler</u>

1. Which of the following captures your reaction to the story of Sabbath on planet Elkon? (Choose one.) Explain.

____   Excited for the future after sin

____   Sad that we still live in a sinful world

____   Worried that I might not make it to the new world God planned for us.

____   Anxious to ask Jesus about His life before sin

____   Intrigued by the portrayal of life on another planet

____   Other:

2. Describe your first Sabbath with Christ in the new earth after sin has been destroyed.

3. Does the size of Christ's universe make you feel more secure or insecure as a Christian? Why?

4. How do you react to the idea that in certain ways we are more like ants than like God?

5. If you were an angel, what would you have said to Christ just before He left heaven to be incarnated in Mary's womb?

6. What helps you the most to picture the awesome side of Christ?

7. As you have traveled through life with God, what parts of the journey have been the most joyful?

Discussion   Questions

Chapter 2   <u>**The Gathering Storm**</u>

1. How did this chapter affect your picture of Christ?

2. What would you be thinking and feeling about Christ if you were a Jewish Passover pilgrim in the Temple when He cleansed it the second time?

3. Which event in this chapter caught your attention the most? Why?

4. "When I see this bold, assertive side of Christ I feel . . ." (choose one). Explain.

____   Comforted
____   Afraid
____   Puzzled
____   Energized
____   Amazed
____   Other:

5. You are one of the twelve disciples. What is going through your mind as you watch Jesus deal with rejection and hate?

6. What can we learn from how Christ dealt with a pressure-cooker life?

7. What storms, big or small, are gathering in your life? How can the group help you?

8. Can you in any way sympathize with the anxiety of the Jewish leaders?

Discussion Questions

Chapter 3   <u>**The Pain of Being Misunderstood**</u>

1. How could the disciples be so thick-headed? If you were born and raised as they were, how do you think you would have reacted to Christ's predictions of His suffering?

2. What messages from God in your own life are the hardest for you to understand?

3. Describe a time when you felt misunderstood. How did you handle it?

4. How could the Jews get so far off track in their expectations of the Messiah? In what ways could that happen to us today in regard to the end time and the second coming?

5. Has God ever come to you in ways you didn't expect? Explain.

6. Think of an area of your life where misunderstandings creep in the most. What can you do to improve that situation in a positive way?

Discussion Questions

Chapter 4   **Physical Torture**

1. You are the disciple John, watching Jesus' trials. What startles you the most?

2. Which one of Jesus' physical sufferings do you personally feel was the most difficult for Him to bear? Why?

3. How has your mental image of Christ as a real-life human being been affected by studying the tortures He endured?

4. Imagine yourself standing at the foot of the cross next to Jesus' mother, Mary. What is going through your mind? What do you say to her?

5. What experience in your own life could help you identify to some degree with Jesus' physical, mental, or spiritual pain?

6. Knowing how offensive and shameful crucifixion was in Jesus' day, how would you witness back then to your pagan Roman neighbor about your Savior who died on a cross?

T H E G I F T

Discussion Questions

Chapter 5   **The News**

1. Which person in this chapter could you identify with the most? Which one do you sympathize with the most? Why?

2. Which person in this chapter made the historical event of Jesus' suffering and death seem more real to you? How?

3. As a follower of Christ, how can you be more than just a spectator in the crowd when you hear of others' pain?

4. If you were a brand-new follower of Christ in A.D. 31 and heard that He had been sentenced to death, would you: (choose one)
____   Stay away until it was safe
____   Seek out other Christians for comfort
____   Try to organize a rescue
____   Be mad at Him for allowing Himself to be taken
____   Follow Him at a safe distance
____   Lose faith in Him
____   Other:

5. When and how did the news of Christ's crucifixion become Good News to you?

6. Tell about some unexpected news that you have received from God in your life?

Discussion Questions

Chapter 6   <u>The Pain of Verbal Abuse</u>

1. Which of the incidents in this chapter affected you the most? In what way?

2. What kinds of verbal abuse do you think hurt Christ the most? Why?

3. "The one word that best captures my reaction to Christ's experience in this chapter is . . ." (choose one). Explain.
____   Surprise
____   Disgust
____   Sympathy
____   Hurt
____   Bewilderment
____   Other:

4. Have you ever been falsely accused of something? How did you react?

5. What kinds of words build up your spirit and what words drag you down?

6. When the devil tries to put you down and oppress your spirit, what helps you the most?

Discussion Questions

Chapter 7   <u>The Pain of Our Own Self-Destruction</u>

1. Tell your own story of something you cherished that was broken or destroyed.

2. What could you do to help restore or improve the natural world that Christ created?

3. How do you react to the statement that "for Him [Christ] just to get out of bed and face each new day took a heroic effort"?

4. "The depth of Jesus' sorrow over the effects of sin tells me that . . ." (choose one) Explain.
_____ He cares very deeply about us
_____ Sin is very destructive
_____ Being God is more painful than I imagined
_____ I need to be more sensitive to other's hurt
_____ Christ fully understands our needs
_____ Other:

5. What aspect of Jesus' sorrow could you identify with the most? Why?

6. What window into the heart of God did this chapter help open for you?

7. Knowing what sorrow tore at Jesus heart, how could He appear so positive? What helps you the most to rise above hurts and sorrow? Give an example.

Discussion Questions

Chapter 8   <u>Forsaken</u>

1. What do you think might have been going through the minds of Peter, James, and John when Jesus awoke them each time in Gethsemane?

2. If you were a newspaper reporter at Calvary between noon and 3:00 P.M. on that fateful Friday, what would you write about in the next issue?

3. What specific experiences in your own life have helped you picture the closeness between Christ and God the Father? Explain.

4. What experiences in your own life, or that of others, can help you appreciate the sense of aloneness Christ endured? In what ways?

5. When you get to heaven, what question would you like to ask Jesus about His experience of being separated from His Father?

6. What is the difference between a church member being simply "religious" and being part of a "love story with God"?

Discussion Questions

Chapter 9   <u>**Releasing the Dragon**</u>

1. Describe a time when you wished you had more protection from danger. What can that tell you about how Jesus might have felt when His angel guard was removed?

2. How would you summarize the various ways that Jesus was affected by the removal of any help from the angels?

3. What tactics did the devil use to oppress Jesus' spirit? Why do you think they were so effective?

4. What is your reaction to Schilder's comment in this chapter that "God did not do much, but He did everything that needed doing; He released the dragon"?

5. What Bible promises would you use to overcome Satan when he comes to you with discouragement and doubt?

6. What dragons are you facing right now that you would like the group to pray about?

Discussion Questions

Chapter 10   A Terrible Silence

1. In what ways has God assured you lately that you are His child and that He is pleased with you?

2. Which of the five assurances do you think meant the most to Christ? Why?

3. Has God ever seemed to you to be a million miles away? How do you deal with that?

4. Why was silence from heaven so difficult for Christ to bear?

5. What word do you think best describes Christ's feelings when the sins of the whole world were laid on Him? (Choose one.) Explain.
____   Fearful
____   Sorrowful
____   Uncertain
____   Anxious
____   Dismayed
____   Overwhelmed

6. How can Jesus' feeling of abandonment help you cope with loneliness in your own life?

7. Like young Rueben, how could you have demonstrated support for Christ on Golgotha?

THE GIFT

Discussion Questions

Chapter 11   Lessons - Part A

1. What insight into the character of God from this chapter was the most helpful to you personally?

2. What misconceptions of God have you had in the past?

3. How would you best describe unconditional love?

4. Do you ever find yourself shying away from God when you fail? What does that tell you about your concept of God?

5. What helps you the most to sense God's love in your own life?

6. Which one of the following differences between human love and God's love means the most to you? (Choose one.) Explain.
____   No strings attached
____   Cannot be earned
____   Gets stronger and stronger
____   Is like the sun
____   Is personal
____   Never gives up

7. Why has the Father so often been seen as the "meany"?

8. What problems arise from the false teaching about God that separates His justice from His love?

Discussion Questions

Chapter 12   <u>Lessons - Part B</u>

1. What lesson in this chapter struck you the most? Why?

2. How do you react to the idea that our sense of worth is God's gift to each of us? What difference could it make if we really believed that?

3. Do you agree that apart from the Holy Spirit we are all capable of acting like the people who treated Christ so badly?

4. Do you have the assurance that by God's grace you are His son or daughter? If not, how can you receive it?

5. Tell about a time when your weakness allowed God to work in a special way.

6. What examples besides Calvary can you give of Jesus' "lion-hearted courage"? How does His bravery in battling the forces of evil give you comfort and hope?